CW01192059

THE SLAVE TRADE

THE SLAVE TRADE

By
Jeremy Black

THE SOCIAL AFFAIRS UNIT

© The Social Affairs Unit 2006
All rights reserved

British Library Cataloguing in Publication Data
A catalogue record of this book is available from the British Library

All views expressed in this publication are those of the author, not those of the Social Affairs Unit, its Trustees, Advisers or Director

Printed and bound in the United Kingdom

ISBN 978-1-904863-22-9

Social Affairs Unit
314–322 Regent Street
London W1B 5SA
www.socialaffairsunit.org.uk

CONTENTS

Preface and Acknowledgements 7

Introduction 9

CHAPTER 1   The Beginnings of the Atlantic Slave
            Trade   21
CHAPTER 2   The Seventeenth Century   37
CHAPTER 3   The Eighteenth Century   61
CHAPTER 4   The Nineteenth Century   97
CHAPTER 5   Legacy and Conclusions   132
Notes   144

For
David and Maggie Armstrong

PREFACE AND ACKNOWLEDGEMENTS

Polls for important books, dates and suchlike are frequently based on a small sample, and that reported in the June 2006 issue of the *BBC History Magazine* on the historical anniversary that ought to be used to celebrate 'British Day' is all too typical. Nevertheless, such polls can be illuminating. The winner, Magna Carta, in fact gained only 1,334 votes, and the second-placed anniversary, VE Day in 1945, only 1,039. In sixth place (with 321 votes) came the abolition of the slave trade in 1807. This was, indeed, an important moment, and one that is likely to be much celebrated in 2007 – and justifiably so. But the bicentenary is also likely to be an occasion for – and, to an extent, the cause of – some contention. It will provide an opportunity for a re-examination of both the slave trade and slavery, but it is likely that some of this re-examination will involve anti-Western diatribes. The strong Arab role in the slave trade before and after 1807 will continue to be widely ignored, because it scarcely suits the anti-Western narrative that so many commentators find convenient for their prejudices. Furthermore, this role is of no use to those who demand reparations from the West. A different, but related, set of flawed assumptions can be seen in references to the Atlantic Middle Passage as 'the African Holocaust'. This asserts an equivalence that did not exist, but also indicates the continuing resonance of the issue, as well as its capacity to strengthen, sustain and court controversy.

A more immediate issue that might invite reflection is the current large-scale attempt by West Africans to reach Europe. Since 2005 these people, mainly young males, have risked their lives travelling long distances in open boats in search of work. There is no ready comparison in scale, intention or brutality with the slave trade, whether across the Atlantic, the Sahara or the Indian Ocean, but the episode serves as a reminder of the difficulties of judging the long-term consequences of migration from Africa.

This book owes its origins to my being invited to edit a four-volume collection of articles and essays, *The Atlantic Slave Trade* (Aldershot: Ashgate, 2006). I am most grateful to John Irwin for asking me to do so. I benefited greatly from being invited by the Division of Continuing Education of the University of Virginia to speak at a conference held in 2000 on 'Jefferson and Slavery', and from the advice of David Aldridge, John Blair, Michael Bregnsbo, Roger Burt, Jan Glete, Christopher Holdsworth, Jim Horn, Thomas Otte, Nigel Ramsay, Joe Smith and Julie Anne Sweet. Bill Gibson kindly commented on an earlier draft. I am most grateful to Clive Liddiard for seeing the book through the press. It is a great pleasure to dedicate this book to a couple who are excellent friends as well as colleagues.

INTRODUCTION

Slavery is one of the most emotive issues in history. To point out that slavery has been a constant for much – possibly all – of human history, and that it has been practised by many societies, is not to minimize the suffering and the impact of the Atlantic slave trade, which did have fundamental effects on Africa, the New World and European imperialism. Nevertheless, it can serve to emphasize that the terrible suffering of the Atlantic trade was not unique, and perhaps ought not to be privileged over other slaveries. These effects reach to the present day – nowhere more so than in the continued relevance of slavery to modern debates about racism and its impact, not least in multiracial societies.[1] The bicentenary, in 2007, of the abolition of the British slave trade will lend historical focus to the discussion.

These debates are, however, in part flawed, because the focus on the Atlantic slave trade leads to a neglect of other such trades. It was a case of multiple slave trades, rather than the Slave Trade. In the Arab world, for example, the slave trade from Africa, both across the Sahara Desert and by sea, across the Indian Ocean and the Red Sea, was more longstanding than in the Atlantic world. Although scholars are aware of the Arab, Ottoman and Indian Ocean dimensions to slavery, this is far less the case with the public debate, whether in Africa, the USA or Western Europe.[2] This trade does not fit with the narrative of Western exploitation, and is therefore widely neglected in public history, as well as in the demand for apology and compensation.

To take the Portuguese as an example: the first of the European slave traders in sub-Saharan Africa in the fifteenth century, they had less of an impact on West Africa than did Moroccan expansionism (just as, in the sixteenth century, they were the first of the European powers to reach the Indian Ocean, yet had much less of an impact on India than the Mughal conquerors of northern India). A Moroccan expeditionary force crossed the Sahara and, in 1591, at Tondibi, used its musketry to defeat the cavalry of Songhai, overthrowing the Songhai empire. In its place, the Moroccans created a Moroccan Pashalik of Timbuktu, which helped strengthen the existing axes for the trans-Saharan slave trade. The folly of writing the history of Africa from the perspective of European pressure is clearly illustrated by an earlier episode, when, in 1578, the Moroccans smashed a Portuguese invading force at Alcazarquivir, killing the king, Sebastian, and ending the longstanding Portuguese attempt to establish a powerful position in Morocco.

Another instance of Islamic pressure on sub-Saharan Africa was provided by Idris Aloma, *mai* (ruler) of Bornu (1569–*c*. 1600), an Islamic state based in the region of Lake Chad. He obtained his musketeers from Tripoli on the Mediterranean, which had been captured from the Knights of St John by the Ottoman Turks in 1551. Similarly, the musketeers and cannon provided by the Ottoman conquerors of Egypt helped Ahmad ibn Ibrihim al-Ghazi in the 1520s to 1540s to sustain his *jihad* in the Horn of Africa (Ethiopia and Somalia) against Christian Ethiopia (which, in turn, as a reminder of the variety of European–African relations, was supported in the early 1540s by Portuguese troops). Indeed the history both of Africa and of its relations with Europe looks very different from the perspective of the Horn of Africa, rather than from the usual perspective of West Africa.

A focus on Ethiopia in the sixteenth century offers a potent reminder that Europeans did not come to Africa simply as oppressors; and, in addition, that there were many among the latter who were not Europeans. Further west, Bornu captured slaves by raiding and, as well as making full use of them itself, transported some of them north, across the Sahara, to the well-established slave markets of North Africa. Bornu was later undermined by the Tuareg, but, to its east, three other states developed in the *sahel* (savannah) belt between the Sahara and the forests further south: Bagirmi, Darfur and Wadai. These states used their military strength to acquire slaves, which they also sent to North Africa.

The slave trade across the Sahara was different from that across the Atlantic for a number of reasons, not least the role of Islam. Furthermore, whereas the prime demand in the Americas was for male labour (which, as a result, ensured a sexual imbalance in local societies affected by the trade[3]), in the case of the trade across the Sahara, the demand was primarily for women, particularly as domestic servants and sex slaves. There was no equivalent in the Islamic world to the large labour-hungry plantation economy of the New World.

In addition to the slave trades across the Atlantic and the Sahara, there were other areas of slaving in Africa: East Africa was a major source of slaves. These were traded across the Red Sea and, further south, the Indian Ocean, to markets in the Middle East, particularly in the Arabian peninsula.

Furthermore, in the centre of Madagascar, the kingdom of Merina, which expanded in the eighteenth century, was given cohesion by a sacred monarchy; force by firearms; and purpose by warfare for slaves. Madagascar was the major source of slaves for the plantations on the French-controlled islands in the Indian Ocean, Réunion and Mauritius, which were, at once, outliers of the Atlantic world and the key to France's presence in the Indian Ocean. As in West Africa, the European territorial presence in Madagascar was very limited, with a French base at Fort Dauphin from 1746 to 1768, and the trade was dependent on African co-operation. For example, Andrianampoinimerina, ruler of Ambohimanga (r. *c.* 1783–*c.* 1810) in the centre of the island, used slaving to acquire guns and gunpowder from the coast where Europeans traded: he seized slaves from other Malagasy territories and exchanged them for the weapons. Having conquered part of the interior, he left his successors to complete the task – a process that produced more slaves. Slavery was part of the labour control that was an aspect of expansionism in Madagascar. Once conquests were made by Andrianampoinimerina's successors, rebellions provoked by demand for forced labour had to be suppressed. Madagascar was not to be conquered by the French until 1894–5.

Lack of sources makes it harder to estimate the number of Africans traded across the Sahara, the Red Sea and the Indian Ocean than across the Atlantic, but it was probably as many – and indeed there are suggestions that it was more.[4] As a further reminder of the variety of the slave trade, and the need for caution in ascribing blame, white slave traders did not provide slaves in the New World exclusively to white owners: in British North America, Native tribes, particularly the Cherokee, owned black slaves from early colonial days, and they were important to Cherokee civilization and prosperity.

Given that the Europeans were far from alone in the slave trade, it is also necessary to query the commonplace identification of slavery with racism. Historically, there was no obligatory relationship between slavery and racism. In medieval Europe, slavery was frequent up to the twelfth century, and slaves were the product of raiding. For example, in Anglo-Saxon England there was slave trading from Ireland. Anticipating the town's prominent role in the African slave trade, many of these slaves were brought ashore at Bristol. In turn, the Vikings based in Dublin took 2,000 prisoners from Anglesey for sale as slaves in Ireland in 987.

Slavery within England was linked with non-membership of the tribe. It declined because of a reduction in the availability of enslavable people, changing patterns of land use, particularly an increase in rented land, and the influence of the Christian religion. It was more economic to give slaves smallholdings so that they became servile tenants. This was often linked with a transition from slaves as single people to servile families. On the smallholdings, it was easier to support families. This ensured that the labour force reproduced itself, which was more useful for the landlord than purchasing slaves. The number of slaves in England probably declined from the early tenth century, although they still formed a substantial group in the Domesday Survey of 1086. By the early twelfth century, slavery, as an institution, was a pale shadow of its former self, although Peterborough Abbey still reported slaves on its estates in the 1120s.[5]

Instead, serfdom became the key form of labour control, which is a reminder of the extent to which slavery was but one alternative among a number of forms of labour control. Serfdom was a system of forced labour based on hereditary bondage to the land. Its purpose was to provide a fixed labour force, and the legal essence of it was a form of personal service to a lord, in exchange for the right to cultivate the soil. Serfdom was used in medieval Europe to provide the mass labour force necessary for agriculture. It entailed restrictions on personal freedom that, in their most severe form, were akin to slavery, and 'many aspects of medieval serfdom were very like slavery'.[6] Serfs were subject to a variety of obligations, principally labour services. They also owed dues on a variety of occasions, including marriage and death. They could also be sold.

Enslavement, nevertheless, remained in Europe, not least as a frequent penalty for illegal behaviour. There were white slaves in the early-modern period, most obviously those who manned the oars of the large numbers of galleys that contested the Turkish advance in the Mediterranean.[7]

Alongside, or despite, this, however, there was a deeper identity of racialism and slavery, for enslavement was frequently the response to the 'other': to other peoples (irrespective of their skin colour), and other creatures. Thus, treating conquered peoples and their offspring as slaves seemed as logical to many as treating animals such as horses as slaves – and also as booty or commodities sold to cover the cost of war. Horses and other beasts of burden were also the creation of God, and therefore part of the divine plan; but the fact that they could be readily subordinated and trained for service to humans apparently demonstrated a natural and necessary fate. In adopting these attitudes, Christian ideology overlapped with Islamic.[8] In a fictional form, the treatment of the 'other' was captured in William Shakespeare's play *The Tempest* (1611), which, in part, drew on accounts of English transoceanic exploration and colonization. In the story, the island's sole inhabitant Caliban, who has an accursed parentage (his father is the Devil, his mother a witch), is enslaved, in turn, by Prospero, a wise but exiled Italian monarch, and then, in response to his exposure to alcohol, by two drunken Italians. Called 'thou poisonous slave' and 'abhorred slave', Caliban is a coerced worker ordered to fetch in wood.

Conflict between cultures increased the possibility of seizing humans as booty, and also eased ideological and normative restrictions on enslavement. This was certainly seen in the European conflict with Islam, with both sides enslaving captives, for example during the Crusades in the Middle East. Similarly, the eastward expansion of Christendom in the Northern Crusades led to the expansion of labour control over non-Germans, such as Pomeranians, Wends, Estonians, Prussians and Livs. Difference was also noted by the law in asserting the legality of slavery. In the case of Butts v. Penny in 1677, the status of a slave was recognized in English law: 'the Court held, the negroes being usually bought and sold among merchants, as merchandise, and also being infidels, there might be a property in them sufficient to maintain trover'. This decision was also followed in Gully v. Cleve (1694), but in 1707, in Smith v. Gould, Sir John Holt, the Lord Chief Justice, decided that 'by the common law no man can have a property in another'. In Smith v. Browne (1701) he had declared that 'as soon as a negro comes to England he is free; one may be a villein [serf] in England but not a slave'.[9]

Among Western Europeans, the Portuguese and Spaniards had the greatest experience of conflict with Islam as a result of the *Reconquista*, in which the Moorish invaders were resisted and then subjugated from the eighth century, the kingdom of Granada finally falling in 1492. This ensured a supply of Moorish slaves, both in Iberia and from the conflict in North-West Africa that overlapped and followed on from the *Reconquista*, Ceuta in Morocco falling to the Portuguese in 1415.

This expansionism was to provide a context within which the opportunities were grasped for enslavement from sub-Saharan Africa. The victims were peoples towards whom there was no traditional antipathy. Portugal led the way in acquiring African slaves in West Africa in the early 1440s, but Castile, the leading Spanish kingdom, followed from 1453 until, in 1479, by the Treaty of Alcáçovas, Castile surrendered its claims to trading rights in Guinea and the Gold Coast to Portugal.

Slavery is like war. In one light, enforced servitude, like large-scale, violent conflict, is easy to define; but, just as discussion of war frequently overlaps with other aspects of conflict and violence, the same is true of slavery, with force and servitude being open to varying definitions. It is hardly necessary to mention the modern term 'wage slave' to make the point that many who are not formally seen as slaves have had little or no choice about work and its character and context, not least in terms of subservience and remuneration. And the point has long been made: in the nineteenth century, for example, during a heated debate, comparisons were drawn – not least, but also not only – by those seeking to extenuate black slavery, between the black slaves in the American South and the white workers in many northern company towns. The latter, in the eyes of critics, were made subservient by various means, including being paid in tokens redeemable only in company shops. Legal freedom thus appeared less important than economic freedom – an issue that Marxists and Southern apologists could both see as pertinent.[10]

In some respects, moreover, slavery can be compared to the serfdom of many Eastern European peasants in the sixteenth to nineteenth centuries.[11] The character of Russian serfdom was bitterly criticized in Alexander Radishchev's book *Journey from St Petersburg to Moscow* (1790), which denounced arduous work, poor living conditions and the right of lords to sell and to flog serfs, all themes also taken up in abolitionist literature.

The slave trade might seem to open up an important distinction between slavery and serfdom: namely the compulsory movement for work in the case of slaves. However, people subject to such movement also included those who were not slaves: transported convicts, others sent to colonies or into internal exile against their will, and even, in one light, the indentured servants and others travelling for economic opportunity within a system in which their choices were limited or non-existent. In 1776, the Scottish economist Adam Smith saw serfdom as a 'milder kind' of slavery.[12]

These complex issues of definition, with the problems of judgment that thereby follow, are not only pertinent for the Western world: they also arise for non-Western societies. For example, the China of the Shang dynasty (1766–1122 BC) has been called a slave society, but it has been argued that this is wrong, since most of the population were not bought or sold, nor were they deprived of their personal freedom, although they were subject to coercive work.[13] Similar points could be made about collective farms under Stalin or about the forced labour imposed in Poland from 1939 – first by the Germans and then by the Soviets.

In advancing a typology of slavery, it is possible to differentiate between societies with slaves (in which slavery was largely a domestic institution providing labour in the household) and slave societies (in which slavery was the mode of production on which the dominant group depended for its position). It is also possible to focus on two types of the latter: slavery at the disposal of the state, and slavery within a private enterprise system. The former tends to receive the least attention, but state slaves of various types were important in many pre-modern countries. In some cases, indeed, they were key elements in the governmental system, most obviously with the janissary units in the Ottoman (Turkish) army, which played a crucial role in the army and the politics of the state until 1826, when, as an aspect of modernization, they were suppressed by Sultan Mahmud II.

Certain modern governments, most obviously North Korea, can be seen to claim so much authority and to wield so much power, and to deny so many freedoms to the people, including that of movement, that their entire population can be regarded as slaves. This point is of wider historical relevance. European political rhetoric in the early-modern period also employed the juxtaposition of liberty and slavery, typecasting as 'slaves' the subjects of political systems judged unacceptable. This was used, for example, by the British against the French, particularly in the wars of the eighteenth century, and was also to be employed by the American Patriots at the time of the American Revolution (1775–83). Radicals who criticized their own system of government made the point repeatedly. Speaking after the abolition of the slave trade by the British government, Arthur Thistlewood, the head of the Cato Street conspiracy to murder the British Cabinet at dinner and seize power, declared at the end of his trial in 1820, 'Albion is still in the chains of slavery. I quit it without regret. My only sorrow is that the soil should be a theatre for slaves, for cowards, for despots.' Such rhetoric is of interest, not least for its contribution to abolitionism, by making it seem a goal for radicals, and also desirable for liberals. Subsequently, such rhetoric itself frequently drew on abolitionism.

However, although there were slaves in Christian Europe during the Middle Ages (and, in the shape of galley slaves, they continued to exist throughout the early-modern period), a characteristic of Western slavery was that it was not a description of the domestic system of government; rather, it was predominantly part of the commercial economy and was generally practised in colonies outside Europe. Slavery in the Western world was a system of servitude, driven essentially by what is termed, without any irony, 'free enterprise'. This provides the crucial context for the slave trade: it was a response to economic need, and a product of the search for economic opportunity. The slave trade was an aspect of the quest for labour – one that was made more necessary by the extent to which labour that could be enslaved or controlled was not obtained in sufficient quantities by conquest. This was in contrast with warfare across much of the world, not only in Africa but also with the expansion of Asian polities. Thus, in Asia, the Mongols in the thirteenth century and the Manchus in the seventeenth acquired slaves by warfare. From the perspective of labour availability, European states and merchants suffered in this quest for labour, since the norms of war did not allow for the enslavement of captives in legitimate warfare between Christian states.

It is appropriate to note here that, co-terminous with the establishment of Western slavery in the New World, rural society in Eastern Europe was transformed towards a 'second serfdom', with heavy-labour services provided by the peasantry. The causes of both developments can be discussed in terms of land–labour ratios.[14] Paralleling the role of plantation exports from the New World, this 'second serfdom' was a response to the commercial opportunities offered by early-modern grain exports to other parts of Europe – an aspect, on the European scale, of what is termed 'globalization'. The 'second serfdom' appears also to have been at least prefigured by fifteenth-century changes, as lords, who had gained private possession of public jurisdictions, responded to the economic problems of the late medieval period, particularly fixed cash incomes.[15] Paralleling the role of landlords in the New World, the attitudes and powers of landlords in Eastern Europe were crucial to the spread of serfdom – not least the character of their seigneurial jurisdiction. The state stood aside or stepped back, and peasant rights were lessened, for example in the Russian legal code of 1649. In another parallel with New World slavery, ethnic divisions, for example between German landlords and Polish peasants, or Polish landlords and Ruthenian and Ukrainian peasants, exacerbated differences in some areas, and were important to the character of this serfdom. Serfdom ended in nineteenth-century Europe, at the same time as slavery came to an end in the Americas.[16]

Western slavery thus represented an aspect of the commodification of human beings for reasons of labour that is central to economic activity. However, focusing modern concerns, it also reflected particular socio-cultural assumptions and practices in which nationhood, religion and, above all, ethnicity, all played important, although varying, roles. These assumptions became operative in particular contexts, and the key context for the modern world was to be European transoceanic expansion. This, however, was not to be the automatic motor for the development of European-controlled slavery – or of a slave trade to sustain it. European expansion also involved the establishment of bases and colonies in a number of areas, from Newfoundland to Java, in which slavery did not become the pattern, although enforced labour, which can be seen as akin to slavery, could still be important, as with the Dutch plantation economy on Java from the seventeenth century. The Russian treatment of the conquered peoples of Siberia was also harsh – particularly, perhaps, the seizure and trading of local women, and the forced tribute in furs, *yasak*.

This variety underlines the fact that European commercial expansionism, like labour exploitation, was not co-terminous with slavery.

CHAPTER 1

THE BEGINNINGS OF THE ATLANTIC
SLAVE TRADE

European slavery was focused on the Atlantic world, rather than on the Indian Ocean, the other major area of European expansion from the cusp of the fifteenth and sixteenth centuries. In essence, this reflected the key role of need, although opportunity was also a factor. In the Indian Ocean world and its outliers, such as the Persian Gulf and the South China Sea, the Europeans did not require large quantities of slave labour, and nor did they have the means to coerce it. European plantation economies did, it is true, develop in this far-flung world, especially under the Dutch in parts of the East Indies (modern Indonesia), and some of these economies used slaves – one example being the French island of Mauritius, with its sugar economy. Nevertheless, most of the goods the Europeans brought back to Europe from the Indian Ocean round the Cape of Good Hope were not produced by slaves and, indeed, were obtained by purchase.

Furthermore, in the case of tea from China, for example, there was no way in which the trade relationship could be altered: despite occasional fantasies of conquest, the Europeans were in no position to dictate to China. As a result, the trade in tea was very different from that in coffee. The ability of the Europeans to establish plantation economies, and to move from trading bases to colonies, was limited around the Indian Ocean and, even more, in the Orient, and this was to be demonstrated further when fortified bases that had been established could not be defended successfully from non-Western attack, as with the Dutch base of Fort Zeelandia on Taiwan in 1662, and the Portuguese bases on the Kanara coast of India in the 1650s, or Fort Jesus at Mombasa in 1698.

The situation was different in the Atlantic world. There, labour was needed and labour was available; just not in the same places. The need for labour sprang from the inherent demographic difference between the Americas and South Asia, from the impact of European expansion following Christopher Columbus's first voyage in 1492, and from the specific labour tasks that the colonists required. In the first case, although this was obviously a pre-census age and there are serious problems with assessing population numbers,[1] there was a major contrast between the percentage of the world's population in the Americas and the much larger percentage in South Asia.

This difference was greatly accentuated by the impact of disease brought by the European invaders of the Americas.[2] This was particularly true of smallpox, which broke out in Mexico in 1520, the year after an invasion force under Hernán Cortés arrived. Smallpox appears to have killed at least half the Aztecs, including their energetic leader Cuitlahuac, and to have hit the morale of the survivors. Disease weakened potential resistance to European control in the Americas, and acted like enslavement in disrupting social structures and household and communal economics, leading to famine. From the European perspective, however, disease also had a savage effect on the potential labour force. The herding together of enslaved peoples, for example Arawaks brought from the Bahamas to work the gold mines of Hispaniola in the 1510s, exacerbated the impact of disease, both new and old. This practice of moving natives to work had already been followed by Spain in the Canaries. Smallpox also decimated the population of Hispaniola, the island subsequently divided between Saint-Domingue, now Haiti, and Santo Domingo, now the Dominican Republic.[3]

More generally, Spanish and Portuguese colonial policies and practices, including the end of Native religious rituals, limited the possibility of post-epidemic population recovery. The Taínos of the Caribbean, for instance, ceased to be a culturally distinct social and ethnic group.[4] All this created acute problems, as the colonists wished to exploit their new possessions, and for this they required labour.

The potential labour force available to the Europeans was also limited by Native resistance. This was to be important in British and French North America from the seventeenth century, but was already apparent in the sixteenth century in what was to become Latin America. From the outset, indeed, the Spaniards had encountered difficulties.[5] They had come to the West Indies via the Canary Islands, which they began to colonize in 1341, seizing the native Guanches (regarded as inferiors) as slaves. The latter, however, mounted a vigorous resistance to Spanish conquest – one that led to numerous Spanish casualties. This conquest has been seen as a conceptual half-way house between the end of the *Reconquista* of Spain and the invasion of the New World.[6]

Vigorous resistance was also a factor in the Americas; but, in the sixteenth and seventeenth centuries, the Spaniards were never in a position to devote the kind of military resources to the New World that they deployed in the much closer and more urgent European and Mediterranean struggles with France and the Ottoman Turks, respectively. While the Spanish conquests of some areas – Cuba (1511–13), central Mexico (1519–21), Peru (1533) and Colombia (1536–9) – were relatively swift, others took far longer. Northward expansion in Mexico was impeded by the Chichimecas in 1550–90 and, further north, by the discovery that there was no gold-rich civilization to loot. The Spaniards also encountered problems in Central America. Cortés himself led a costly campaign in Honduras in 1524. Guatemala was conquered by 1542, but, although much of the Yucatán, the centre of Mayan civilization, was conquered in 1527–41, the Itzás of the central Petén were not defeated until 1697.[7] In some areas, such as southern Chile, the Spaniards were never successful, ensuring that relations between the Natives and the Spanish were not defined simply by the control exercised by the latter. The first Spanish fort at St Augustine in Florida, built in 1565, was burned down by the Timucua the following spring.[8]

Similarly, in Brazil, which they 'discovered' and claimed in 1500, the Portuguese made only slow progress in extending control in the interior at the expense of the Tupinambá and Tapuya, although they were helped by rivalries between tribes and, indeed, by alliances with some. Portuguese muskets were of little value against the nomadic Aimoré, mobile warriors who were expert archers and well adapted to forest warfare.[9]

After the initial conquest stage on the mainland in the first half of the sixteenth century, Spanish and Portuguese territorial expansion in the Americas slowed down. This had major implications for labour supply. Natives who were willing to supply goods to the Europeans by barter were not prepared to provide continuous labour on plantations. As an alternative way of obtaining labour, raiding was more common than the purchase of Native slaves. It was possible to seize labour by mounting raids into unconquered areas, and this widespread practice continued for centuries, though it was far from easy.[10] The populations either fled before the raiders or resisted them, with a major rebellion in the leading Brazilian sugar-producing area in 1567. This illustrates clearly that the slave trade was, at least in part, shaped by the responses of non-Europeans. In addition, some of the areas into which raids were conducted, for example the interior of Brazil, were distant from the coastal centres of agriculture. Native slaves, nevertheless, were important in frontier regions distant from the points of arrival of African slaves, such as Amazonia and northern Mexico.

Alongside supply problems, control over Native labour within the area of Spanish control was affected by royal legislation, which sought to address clerical pressure to treat the Natives as subjects ready for Christianization, rather than as slaves. As a result, following the 1477 decision by Queen Isabella of Castile to order the freeing of those Natives from the Canaries who had been sold as slaves in Castile, Native slavery was formally abolished in the *Leyes Nuevas* of 1542. The Portuguese government followed with legislation in 1609.[11]

The implementation of edicts, however, took time and was frequently ignored by local officials and landowners. Moreover, systems of tied labour, especially the *encomienda* (land and Native families allocated to colonists), and forced migration (notably the *repartimiento*, under which a part of the male population had to work away from home) represented *de facto* slavery. They certainly led to a caste system, based on ethnicity, that has played a key role in Latin American history, and that has become more important in the recent politics of the area, not least in the latest elections in Bolivia, Peru and Mexico.[12]

Nevertheless, the difficulty of ensuring sufficient numbers of malleable workers encouraged the import of labour from the Old World. Initially, labour needs were partially supplied by Moors, captured in the conflicts that were so frequent in the fifteenth and sixteenth centuries. Similarly, Portuguese peasants were moved to Brazil. These resources, however, proved to be only limited, not least on account of Portuguese and Spanish failure in North Africa in the sixteenth century.

Instead, in the Spanish New World, from the 1510s, reliance was placed on the spread of African slavery. Unlike later on, initially this had little to do with tackling the labour problems created by the death of much of the Native population in the West Indies; at this stage, the Spaniards satisfied such labour needs primarily from other Caribbean islands. This process was extended to the mainland, where there was large-scale slaving among Natives in Honduras and Nicaragua. The former was to satisfy demand in the Caribbean, and the latter was mainly for Peru, though also for Panama and the Caribbean. This method of labour provision was later extended to North America.[13]

Initially, Africans were shipped into Spanish America via Spain, but in 1518 *asientos*, or licences, were granted for the import of slaves direct from Africa to Spanish America. African slavery was widely regarded by European thinkers as justified in natural law. As it was initially more expensive to supply Spanish America with African slaves, who had to be purchased in Africa and brought across the Atlantic, than with Native slaves, the Africans were often used as house slaves, a form of high-value slavery that indicated their cost. As a reminder from the outset of the variety of roles that Africans were to take in the Americas, some fought as conquistadors.[14] Such variety undercut racial typecasting, but far less so than it should have done.

By the mid-sixteenth century, the situation had changed and, rather than providing a marginal part of the labour force, Africa was becoming steadily more important as a source of slaves, not least because it was believed that Africans were physically stronger than Natives. Nevertheless, African slaves remained more expensive than Native labour. The latter could be controlled in various ways, including by making service an element of debt repayment. In 1570, there were probably only 20,000 African slaves in Spanish America,[15] and less than five per cent of the total number of slaves 'exported' from Africa in the Atlantic trade between 1450 and 1900 were moved prior to 1600. Particularly from the mid-sixteenth century, however, the trend was upwards, reflecting demand from both Spanish and Portuguese colonies.

African slaves were used for a variety of tasks across Spanish America. In some areas, agricultural work was important, usually for cash crops, such as sugar in the valleys of northern Peru and wine on the Peruvian coast. Profits from such crops covered the cost of purchasing slaves. In Peru, Africans were judged more suited to the heat and humidity of the coastal valleys than Native Americans, who were generally used in the higher and drier terrain with which they were more familiar. As a result, the slave trade was part of the process by which Europeans reconceptualized and responded to the geography and demographics of the areas they conquered. Slaves were also used to produce food destined to be sold to the cities and to the mine towns, such as the great silver-producing centre of Potosi, which was a crucial source of bullion for the Spanish empire and the European trading system. Mine towns were another area of employment for slaves, although the prime labour supply there was from Native

Americans, and Africans, as a reflection of their higher value, tended to be used in refining and as overseers. In the cities, slaves were employed in various roles, including as craftsmen, servants and labourers.[16]

Blacks remained a smaller group than Native Americans across most of Spanish America. In central Mexico, the percentage of the population who were Natives in 1646 was 87.2, while Spaniards, whether born in Mexico or immigrants, amounted to eight per cent, *mestizos* (mixed) were 1.1 per cent, and *pardos* (wholly or partly black) 3.7 per cent. In the mid-1740s, the respective percentages were 74 and then about nine each, while as far as the whole of Mexico was concerned, the population in 1810 has been estimated at about 6,121,000: 3,676,000 Natives, 1,107,000 Spaniards, 704,000 *mestizos* and 634,000 *pardos*.[17] However, where disease had really ravaged the Native population, for example in Puerto Rico and Hispaniola, the black population by 1600 was greater than that of the surviving Taínos.

In Brazil, also, the initial emphasis was on the use of Native labour, just as, in the Canaries, the Guanches had initially been used as slaves on the sugar plantations. However, in Brazil, as sugar cane was introduced and became more important, it proved necessary to supplement slave raiding into the interior with the import of slaves from West Africa and Angola, in both of which the Portuguese had bases. Indeed, the Portuguese also used slaves in their plantations in Angola. The Native slave population of Portuguese Brazil was hit hard by a smallpox epidemic in 1560–3 and a measles epidemic in 1563. As a result, short of labour for the sugar economy, in the last quarter of the century Brazil imported about 40,000 African slaves.[18]

It is instructive to consider demand before supply, because that explains how Europeans created and responded to opportunities in Africa, with the creation and the response frequently proving to be closely linked, if not two sides of the same coin. Portuguese expeditions along Africa's Atlantic coast in the fifteenth century had been motivated primarily by a search for gold, rather than for slaves. Among the illustrations on the African portion of the *Catalan Atlas* of 1375 was a depiction of the fabled king of Mali, Mansa Munsa. The text read: 'So abundant is the gold in this country that the lord is the richest and noblest king in all the land.' Legend had it that Mali possessed dazzling quantities of gold. The 1413 map by Mecia de Viladestes reflected the expansion of knowledge about West Africa as European explorers moved south. This map also reflects the interest in trading into the West African interior to obtain gold and other goods without the intermediacy of the North African Muslims. It did not prove easy for the Portuguese to gain access to the gold, which was dominated by the Waranga. Gold, instead, was exchanged for salt from the Saharan salt mines that was brought by Moorish traders using camels, some of which were then eaten.[19] The Portuguese, nevertheless, did gain entry into the gold trade, although, from 1441, the sale of slaves brought from Africa either to Portugal or to its colony of Madeira also became important. The Portuguese first met black Africans in Senegambia, the region from the mouth of the River Senegal to that of the River Gambia, and it was from there that the first slaves came. The gold of West Africa obtained from the River Gambia and the Gold Coast also acted as a major spur for the slave trade, because slaves acquired elsewhere on the coast became useful as something to sell in exchange for gold.[20] The gold trade of São Jorge da Mina (Elmina) on the Gold Coast was controlled as a royal monopoly.[21]

Slaves were also used as a labour force in Portugal, Africans feeding into the pattern already established for Moors. From the 1440s on, the Portuguese exported significant numbers of slaves from Africa, with between 140,000 and 170,000 slaves imported into Portugal itself between 1441 and 1505, most working in domestic service or on the sugar plantations of Madeira.[22]

In time, the gold and slave economy was to be transformed into a slave economy. This reflected labour needs, especially the demands of sugar production, which ensured that Brazil came rapidly to play a key role in the trans-Atlantic slave trade. Sugar production had been developed within the European world in the Atlantic islands: Madeira, the Azores, the Cape Verde islands and the Canaries. Portuguese settlement of Madeira began in 1424, of the Azores in 1427, and of the Cape Verde Islands in the late 1450s, and it was from there that the plantation system was transferred to Hispaniola in 1503 and to Brazil in the 1530s.[23]

Brazil rapidly supplanted Madeira as the leading producer of sugar in the Portuguese world, enjoying as it did a comparative advantage due to slave labour, as well as relatively fresh soil in plentiful quantities.[24] This enabled Portugal to benefit from its new colony. The number of sugar mills in Brazil rose from 60 in 1570 to 192 in around 1600. North-East Brazil, the centre of sugar production, where there was a lengthy harvest season and relatively mild weather, was close to Africa.

This is a reminder of how oceans could link rather than separate: it is rather artificial to use continents, i.e. landmasses, to define space. Indeed, as a result of the development of links in the Atlantic economy, West Africa was, in some respects, to become closer to Brazil than it was, for example, to South-East Africa.

Relatively short slaving voyages were particularly valuable, because they reduced the need for credit in bridging the period between the purchase and the sale of slaves. Death rates among the slaves were also generally lower on shorter voyages. In the 1570s, the number of Africans among the slaves in North-East Brazil increased, so that, by the mid-1580s, about one third of slaves were Africans; by 1620 they were in a majority. The slave population of Brazil rose from about 15,000 in 1600 to about 150,000 in 1680. The slave trade provided royal revenues to the Crown of Portugal: aside from slaves moved on the royal account, private slave traders were taxed.

In both Brazil and Spanish America, the high death rate and low fertility rate of African slaves once they arrived – rates that reflected the cruel hardships of enslavement, transport and labour – ensured that it was necessary to import fresh slaves in order to sustain the numbers required. This affected the nature of slave society, sustaining its African character – for example, the traditional pattern of marriage customs, religious beliefs and related ideas about kin and family, and thus its foreignness to Native societies.[25]

The Atlantic slave trade from Africa was a new variant on the longstanding pattern of slavery and slave trade within Africa – a pattern that is, however, relatively obscure. There is a need to emphasize the word 'variant', because there is room to suppose that the possibilities of trade encouraged new ways of exploiting existing patterns of social stratification and dependency. At the same time, slave-owning and hierarchical monarchies did not originate at the time of the Atlantic slave trade, but were in evidence in parts of Africa, for example the western Sudan, from the eleventh century, if not earlier. This, however, might suggest not indigenous origins, but, rather, the impact of the trans-Saharan slave trade.

It is unclear how far labour shortages in Africa encouraged enslavement as a means of securing labour (a system analogous to the 'second serfdom' in Eastern Europe), and how far this system then helped provide slaves to European traders. The issue is related to the extent to which slaves were a form of wealth: both a source and a symbol of wealth – in part because they were scarcer than land, which only took on value when it was farmed. Furthermore, as a result, Africans could readily commodify slaves for use in barter and as money. The majority of Africans who were sold as slaves were captured in warfare, but some were also enslaved as a result of judicial punishment.[26] Those who were captured thus lost their tribal identity, and this was an aspect of slavedom. The situation was similar among certain other societies, for example the Maori of New Zealand.

On the west coast of Africa, the Europeans obtained slaves by trading, and the business was initially conducted either from on board the slave ships anchored in estuaries or on the coast. The Europeans were not powerful enough to seize slaves using the large-scale raiding technique employed in Central America and Brazil. The Portuguese initially did favour this method, but abandoned it in the late 1440s because the rulers of Upper Guinea south of the River Senegal were too strong.[27] The Portuguese, indeed, faced a variety of serious problems in Africa – problems that qualify the sense of European military superiority. African coastal vessels, powered by paddles and carrying archers and javelin-men, were able to challenge Portuguese raiders on the West African coast. Although it was difficult for them to storm the larger, deeper-draught and higher-sided Portuguese ships, they were too fast and too small to present easy targets for the Portuguese cannon. In 1535, for example, the Portuguese were once more repelled when they tried to conquer the Bissagos Islands off the West African coast.

Furthermore, disease was as debilitating for the Europeans in Africa as it was for their Native opponents in the New World. About 60 per cent of the Portuguese soldiers who served in Angola in 1575–90 died of disease. Most of the rest were killed or deserted. In addition, horses could not survive. This was not only a problem in Angola: in West Africa, the average annual death rate among the agents of the British Royal African Company between 1684 and 1732 was 270 per 1,000.[28]

Moreover, prevailing wind and ocean conditions limited access to the African coast south of the Gulf of Guinea, while the extensive coastal lagoons and swamps of West Africa made access to the coastline difficult. Penetration inland was variously hindered by tropical rainforest and, on the coasts of modern Mauritania and Namibia, by desert conditions.

More generally, the environment was far more difficult for European conquest than in much of the New World. Whereas Mexico and Peru were populous and had a well-developed agricultural system that could provide plenty of resources for an invader, Africa lacked comparable storehouses, food for plunder, and roads. Mexico and Peru were also more centralized politically, and thus easier to take over once the ruler had been seized. In contrast, Africa was more segmented, and new chiefs could emerge. This helped encourage the conflict within the continent that fed the slave trade, but neither conflict nor slavery was dependent on the

European presence. In the sixteenth century, this was true, for example, of the destruction in West Africa of Mali by the Songhai Empire in 1546, and of the subsequent overthrow of the latter in turn by the Moroccans; and also, in the Horn of Africa, of the destructive attacks on Adal and Ethiopia by the pagan Galla from the Ogaden.

Rather than conquest, trade was a more successful means of European access to Africa, and it also helped to finance further expansion. The profits from the trading base of São Jorge da Mina, founded in 1482, financed later voyages, such as those of Diogo Cão and Bartolomeu Dias. Indeed, the possibilities of the slave trade led, in 1486, to the establishment of the *Casa dos Escravos de Lisboa* (Lisbon Slave House). Mina itself was a logistical achievement, prefabricated with stores, timbers and tiles all prepared in Portugal. Later Portuguese bases included Axim (1495), Accra (1515) and Shama (1526), and, off the coast, Fernando Póo (1483).[29]

In 1483, Diogo Cão became the first European to set foot in the kingdom of Kongo. Peaceful relations were established, and, in 1491, the king was baptized João I. A syncretic blend of Christianity and local religious elements spread rapidly, a syncretism that is a good model for much of the more general process of European impact in Africa, although, conversely, Christian conversion on this scale did not occur elsewhere, despite attempts in Sierra Leone in the early seventeenth century.

The Portuguese were leaders in the slave trade to and from the sub-Saharan coasts of Africa, not least because the Spaniards ceased to be traders there in 1479. This withdrawal reflected, in part, what was to be the longstanding Spanish willingness to purchase slaves from others, with licences given to the Portuguese to import slaves into the New World; and, in part, their ability to secure slaves in the Americas, including from the children of slaves and from raiding among the Native American population. The coerced labour of the subject Native population was also important.

The Portuguese position in West Africa was challenged by the English in the mid-sixteenth century, from the reign of the

Catholic Mary I (r. 1553–8). The pioneers of English slavery were merchants based in lower Andalusia in Spain at the end of the fifteenth century and beginning of the sixteenth, with William de la Founte, in 1490, proving the earliest documented English slave holder there. At a very different level, Henry VII (r. 1485–1509) kept some black domestic servants. The first recorded English colonist in Hispaniola was Nicholas Arnold in 1508.[30]

The English subsequently made an attempt to break into Portugal's trade with West Africa, and the profitable slave trade between there and the Spanish New World. John Hawkins, who obtained his slaves in West Africa by raiding, rather than through purchase (losing men in the process to poison arrows and other hazards), sold slaves to the Spaniards.[31] However, in 1568, on his third slaving voyage, at San Juan de Ulúa near Vera Cruz in modern Mexico, the presence of the Viceroy of New Spain led to a Spanish attack on what was, in the official view, an unwelcome interloper. This contributed to the large loss made by the venture; only two English ships survived the attack.[32]

The unwillingness of Elizabeth I (r. 1558–1603), in the early years of her reign, to confront directly the imperial interests of Portugal and Spain encouraged a reliance on unofficial or semi-official action, such as privateering. England did not go to war with Spain until 1585. By then, Portugal's position had changed, because, in 1580, Philip II of Spain became also Philip I of Portugal, backing up his claim to the throne with one of the most rapid and decisive military campaigns of the century. This dynastic link continued until a successful rebellion in Portugal in 1640. As a result, it was possible for those at war with Spain, such as the English and the Dutch, to breach the Portuguese monopoly without fear of admonition from their home governments.

In the late sixteenth century, however, the English commitment to the slave trade was far less than it was to be in the seventeenth century. In this period, most English voyages to West Africa were for pepper, hides, wax and ivory, and in search of gold rather than of slaves. No English fort was built in West Africa in this period. English trade with West Africa did not focus on the slave trade until the mid-seventeenth century.[33] The Dutch, initially, also played only a modest role in the trade. They were subjects of Philip II of Spain and, after they rebelled in the 1560s, were primarily concerned with the war for their independence and the naval struggle in home waters. However, later, in 1594, Philip II banned Dutch trade with Lisbon, which encouraged the Dutch to look further afield. France in the late sixteenth century was consumed by civil war in the form of the French Wars of Religion. This did not prevent the French attempting to get established in the New World, but they were unsuccessful in this period. Although they burnt Havana in 1552, their attempts to establish themselves in Florida were defeated by the Spaniards. French attempts to found bases in Brazil – in 1555 on the site of modern Rio de Janeiro and in 1558 at São Luís in northern Brazil – proved short-lived. In the Caribbean, Spanish defensive measures improved in the sixteenth century and, as a result, in 1595–6, Sir Francis Drake's last Caribbean expedition was a failure.

The greater experience in long-distance, deep-sea voyaging and commerce gained in the sixteenth century provided important background to the later expansion of the slave trade. This rested on a significant improvement in the capability of shipping, which gave the Europeans a powerful comparative advantage. Late fourteenth- and fifteenth-century developments in ship construction and navigation included the fusion of Atlantic and Mediterranean techniques of hull construction and lateen- and square-rigging, the spread of the sternpost rudder, and advances in location-finding at sea. Carvel building (in which hull planks are fitted flush together over a frame), which spread from the Mediterranean to the Atlantic from the late fifteenth century, replaced the clinker method of shipbuilding using overlapping planks, and contributed significantly to the development of the stronger and larger hulls necessary for trade across the Atlantic. The increase in the number of masts on large ships expanded the range of choices for rigging and provided a crucial margin of safety in the event of damage to one mast. Developments in rigging, including an increase in the number of sails per mast and in the variety of sail shapes, permitted greater speed, a better ability to sail close to the wind and improved manoeuvrability.[34]

Navigational expertise also increased. Thanks to the use of the magnetic compass, the spread from the Mediterranean to Atlantic Europe of astrolabes, cross-staffs and quadrants (which made it possible to assess the angle in the sky of heavenly bodies) and other developments in navigation, such as the solution in 1484 to the problem of measuring latitude south of the Equator, it became possible to chart the ocean and to assemble knowledge about it. This was an important prelude to the further development of the slave trade, not least because better charts helped reduce the risk of voyaging, and thus the hazards of sailing.[35] In 1516, the explorer Amerigo Vespucci's nephew, Juan, was instructed to produce a *pardon real* (official royal chart), a work that was frequently updated to take note of new reports from navigators.

Columbus's pilot on his second voyage, Juan de la Cosa, is usually held to have produced the first map to show the discoveries, but it may have appeared later than the traditional date of 1500. In 1502, the Cantino map depicted the Americas, and also West Africa, the coast of which was revealed in greater detail. The interior of Africa, however, was largely unknown. Giacomo Gastaldi's eight-sheet map of Africa, published in Venice in 1564 and the largest map of Africa yet to appear, reflected journeys into the interior – for example, those of the Portuguese into Ethiopia – but also depicted non-existent large lakes. The *Descrittione dell' Africa* (Venice, 1550), by the Arab scholar known as Leo Africanus, was an important source for European mapping, but his errors included the idea that the River Niger flowed westwards, a belief linked to the conviction that a large lake must be its source.

In 1569, Gerard Mercator, a Flemish mathematician, produced a projection that treated the world as a cylinder, so that the meridians were parallel, rather than converging on the poles. Taking into account the curvature of the Earth's surface, Mercator's projection kept angles, and thus bearings, accurate in every part of the map. A straight line of constant bearing could thus be charted across the plane surface of the map, a crucial tool for navigation. As the shape of the world was increasingly grasped, so the opportunities for profit appeared more realizable. The growth in trans-Atlantic trade, in goods and slaves, was to reflect this. As the trade became more regular and predictable, so it became more dependable as a source of labour.

In turn, this growth in the slave trade fortified the perception and treatment of sub-Saharan Africans as slaves. 'Blackness' had proved a slippery concept for Europeans, who tended to see some of their own number as dark-skinned. As a result of the slave trade, however, black Africans were stereotyped and many African cultural practices were misunderstood and recast in a negative light. Denigration as inferior and uncivilized was related to pigeonholing in occupations linked to physical prowess and thus to slavery.[36] The same process took place in the Arab world. The relationship between such attitudes and the grasping of economic opportunity is a complex one. In this chapter, I have downplayed the former by drawing attention to the widespread nature of unequal, and frequently coerced, labour relationships in this period. This is a theme of the book. It does not, and should not, serve to downplay the horrors of slavery, but, instead, to contextualize them.

CHAPTER 2

THE SEVENTEENTH CENTURY

The major growth in the Atlantic slave trade in the seventeenth century was to be driven by the expansion of New World exports to Europe, and it is appropriate to begin with the geopolitics of these economic forces, rather than with the process of European colonization. Labour demands ensured that growth was required in the case of plantation crops, particularly sugar, tobacco and coffee, but not in the case of cod exports from Newfoundland, for example.

The export from the Americas of plantation crops, together with the export to the Americas of the European manufactured goods that this helped finance, played a major role in restructuring much of the European economy. This two-way trade powerfully developed and accentuated the role of Europe's Atlantic seaboard, and crucially strengthened the importance of port cities, particularly Bordeaux and Bristol, Liverpool and Nantes. The import of plantation crops also greatly affected the material culture of Europeans, their diet and health. By supplying new products, or providing existing ones at a more attractive price, or in new forms, this trade both satisfied and stimulated consumer demand.

Transoceanic trade provided Europeans with goods designed to stimulate: sugar, tobacco and caffeine drinks – tea (from Asia), coffee and chocolate.[1] As none of these was 'necessary', this was very much consumerism, and one linked to shifts in taste. Sugar came to be much more important to the response of individuals to food and drink, partly replacing honey as a sweetener in cooking and drinks. Sugar had been a luxury: when, in 1603, James VI and I's daughter, Elizabeth, came south from Scotland with her father, she was presented with a sugar loaf at York. Demand for sugar, however, interacted with a rapidly rising supply from the Americas, and this led to the average retail price of sugar falling considerably in the second half of the century, which greatly encouraged demand. This development made the trade more predictable, which encouraged more investment; that, in turn, led to further downward pressure on prices.

Taste, as well as price, was at issue. The addition of sugar to drinks increased their popularity by making them easier on the European palate, while the rising consumption of caffeine drinks increased demand for sugar. Chocolate was altered by sugar, making it a sweet rather than a bitter drink. This made chocolate as a drink more popular in Europe and encouraged the growth in export there of its main ingredient, cacao. Sugar was also added to jam, cakes, biscuits and medicine.

Much cacao was obtained by the Spaniards from the Native population, but this was supplemented by plantation production. The French established cacao plantations on their colonies of Martinique and Guadeloupe in the West Indies in the early 1660s, the Portuguese followed in Brazil in the late 1670s, and the Dutch (in Surinam) and the English (on Jamaica, but with limited success) in the 1680s. As the production of cacao increased, so prices fell, and this encouraged consumption.[2]

As with sugar and other plantation crops, the development of cacao production helped drive the slave trade. The sale of cacao from the Spanish-ruled Venezuelan coast began in the 1610s and encouraged the import of African slaves there. This cacao was sold to Spanish markets in the Americas – a reminder of the variety of the Atlantic economy, in which slavery played such a dynamic role. In the 1630s and 1640s, rising cacao sales from Venezuela helped finance larger slave imports there. On average, each adult slave generated about 40 per cent of their market value each year, which was a very high rate of return. Initially, the slaves were provided by the Portuguese; but, from mid-century, the Dutch, based on the nearby island of Curaçao, became more important. The mobility of the slave gangs helped expand the frontier of production, and by 1744 there were over five million cacao trees in the Caracas province. In contrast, the *encomienda* system, and the use of the Native American population it offered, was of limited use in satisfying new labour demand.[3]

Sugar was also profitable, particularly when special opportunities beckoned. These were usually a matter of war between producers. On the English colony of Barbados, for example, in the 1650s profits of as much as 40 or 50 per cent reflected the impact of the lengthy mid-century war in Brazil on competing Dutch and Portuguese sources of sugar imports into Europe.[4] Sugar also meant slaves. Initially, settlers in the English West Indian colonies had largely been labourers provided by contracts of indenture, a practice of labour provision and control transplanted from England. Plantation work, however, was hard, ensuring that labour availability and control were key issues. The labour regime in sugar and rice cultivation was particularly arduous and deadly; production of tobacco and cacao was less so. Hacking down sugar cane – crucial to the production process – was backbreaking work. It also required a large labour force, and slavery provided this more effectively than indentured labour, which was not only less malleable but also less attuned to the environment in the West Indies, in particular the climate. The impact in the late 1640s of disease on the white settlers encouraged this process.[5] Captain William Freeman, who, from 1670, developed a sugar plantation on the English colony of Montserrat in the West Indies, claimed that 'land without slaves is a dead stock'.[6]

Colonies that shifted from tobacco (the price of which slumped in the 1640s) to sugar saw a marked increase in the slave population and less of a reliance on indentured labour: on Montserrat, 40 per cent of the 4,500-strong population in 1678 was non-white; but this had grown to 80 per cent of the 7,200-strong population by 1729.[7] The same process occurred on other islands, such as Barbados, which was hit by a falling supply of white servants. Instead, these servants were now attracted to South Carolina, Virginia and Maryland.[8]

This shift drove the slave trade to the English West Indies. Slaves suddenly appeared in Barbados deeds in 1642, following the arrival of the first English slave ships there the previous year. Although the prices of slaves thereafter fluctuated annually, they did generally decline over time.[9] This encouraged the trade and reflected its more sophisticated organization, which was at once responsive to both sources and markets. Price was not the only factor in encouraging the use of slaves: they also ensured a longer labour availability than that provided by indentured servants.[10]

On Jamaica, another English colony, the black population rose to 42,000 in 1700, when there were only 7,300 whites. Jamaica switched from smallholdings to plantation monoculture. During this period, slave buying was widespread among the white community, but large purchasers dominated the market, which reflected their access to credit and also accentuated social stratification. The market became more complex and came to be controlled by specialized traders. Important to this complexity and specialization was a growing resale market within Jamaica that further accentuated the instability of the slaves' lives.[11] The numerical relationship between slaves and whites led the latter to support garrisoning by soldiery, and the removal of soldiery for whatever reason alarmed the whites. The sense of alarm was communicated to European readers by publications such as *Great Newes from the Barbadoes, or, A True and faithful account of the grand conspiracy of the Negroes against the English and the happy discovery of the same* (1676).

All too often, the slave trade is seen in terms of the North Atlantic, but the South Atlantic trade was crucial,[12] and should be discussed first, not least in order to challenge the focus on the North Atlantic. From the 1570s, sugar production developed rapidly in Portugal's colony of Brazil, producing a 'white gold' economy. This was based on slave labour, initially from Senegambia in West Africa, the part of sub-Saharan Africa where the Portuguese had first arrived, but later increasingly from the Portuguese colony of Angola. Sugar production helped ensure that Brazil received 42 per cent of the slaves imported into the Americas during the seventeenth century, the largest individual flow by colony. The number of slaves arriving in Brazil exceeded the number of white settlers. This flow was necessary because, on the sugar estates of Brazil, slaves had a life expectancy of up to eight years only, a grim reality that reflected the arduous nature of the work there and the harshness of the conditions. Luso-African slaving networks, rather than the government, provided the capital, dominated the supply, and took the profit, and these networks linked the African interior to the Atlantic coast, where, in 1616, a new port was opened at Benguela in Angola to support the trade. It was to take second place to Luanda as the port for the Angolan slave trade.

The Dutch attempt to conquer Brazil from the 1620s, however, greatly disrupted sugar production there, not least because the Dutch focused on North-East Brazil, capturing Recife in 1630. This disruption led to a marked shift in production to the West Indies, a process accentuated when Dutch failure in Brazil from 1645 was followed in 1654 by the recapture of Recife and the expulsion of Dutch and Jewish settlers from Brazil. They brought to the Caribbean their capital, mercantile contacts, and expertise in sugar-mill technology. On the other side of the Atlantic, the Dutch had also captured the Portuguese slaving bases of Luanda, Benguela and São Tomé in 1641, affecting the availability of slaves in Brazil. This encouraged slave hunting in the Brazilian interior. In 1648, however, a Portuguese fleet from Brazil recaptured these positions.[13]

This provided the basis for a marked revival of the integrated Portuguese slave and sugar economy in the South Atlantic. The profitability of Brazil, in turn, meant that the Portuguese Atlantic empire did not suffer from the lack of capital and relative uncompetitiveness seen in Portuguese Asia,[14] and this ensured that the slave trade could serve to accumulate capital and provide an opportunity for fresh investment.

Dutch slave exports to Brazil were affected by the Portuguese victory, which helped ensure that the Dutch increasingly focused instead on Spanish America, using their Caribbean base of Curaçao as an entrepôt; their island of St Eustatius was another. The Dutch also supplied slaves to their colonies in the Guianas: Essequibo, Demerara (where New Amsterdam was founded in 1627) and Surinam (where Paramaribo was founded in 1613). They competed with England on this coast, especially in Essequibo and Surinam. Meanwhile, further east, Cayenne, the basis of French Guiana, was founded as a colony in 1635.

France, England and the Dutch also all acquired bases further north. As well as Cayenne, the French settled a number of islands in the West Indies – St Christopher (St Kitts, 1625), Martinique (1635), Guadeloupe (1635), Dominica (1635), Grenada (1650) and Saint-Domingue (now Haiti, 1660) – as well as Louisiana. Claimed by La Salle in 1682, this last had its first French base at Fort Maurepas in Biloxi Bay on the Gulf of Mexico coast of the modern state of Mississippi in 1699. The French also established bases on the coast of Africa, St Louis in 1638, Gorée in 1677 and Assinie in 1687 becoming bases for slavers.

The British, at this stage the English, established settlements on islands that the Spaniards had not colonized, although this was no easy matter. Settlements were founded on St Lucia in 1605 and Grenada in 1609, but opposition from native Caribs contributed to their failure. This provided a valuable instance of the folly of assuming that there was a Western military superiority on land, or that the West automatically carried all before it. Bermuda, an island in the Atlantic, remote from other islands, was discovered in 1609 and inspired Shakespeare's play *The Tempest*. Settled in 1612, Bermuda became a successful colony, where tobacco cultivation was swiftly introduced. The first black slaves arrived in 1616. After Bermuda came the establishment of lasting English colonies on Barbados in 1627, Nevis in 1628 and Antigua and Montserrat in 1632, although an attempt upon the Spaniards on Trinidad in 1626 failed. These colonies were no mere adjunct to the English possessions in North America. Instead, they generated more wealth and, until the

1660s, attracted more settlers than the possessions on the North American mainland, Barbados proving the most popular destination.

Buccaneering and contraband trade remained important in the English colonies. Indeed, on Jamaica, these activities helped provide much of the initial capital that financed plantation agriculture.[15] More settled activity also developed. The islands were rapidly used for commercial agriculture, and the labour-intensive nature of the resulting plantation economies led to a need for settlers. Sugar was to lead to slaves, and, in particular, the replacement of tobacco smallholdings by sugar plantations; but it is important not to regard this as the inevitable economic and social pattern of the colonies in the West Indies. Sugar was not the sole plantation crop there in the late seventeenth century: on Jamaica, the English also had cacao, cotton, ginger and indigo plantations. Moreover, a more mixed, less capital-intensive economic pattern was initially dominant, and it continued to be important even after the emphasis came to be placed on sugar, although sugar did dominate exports.[16] Similarly, the use of slaves in Spanish American agriculture was not simply linked to export agriculture.

The English presence in the West Indies was expanded by the settlement of Jamaica (the largest English colony there) and the Cayman Islands from 1655, the Virgin Islands from 1666, and the Bahamas from 1670. Much of the immigration by both white migrants and slaves was, however, to already established colonies such as Barbados. Expansion took place within a system made dynamic by conflict. The value of plantation exports encouraged the European powers to try to seize each other's positions, although they were frequently unsuccessful. Thus, the Dutch failed to take Martinique from the French in 1674, and the French could not wrest Curaçao from the Dutch in 1678. The English Western Design of 1654–5 against the Spanish colony of Hispaniola failed, England unsuccessfully attacked Guadeloupe in 1691 and Martinique in 1693, and failed to capture Saint-Domingue in 1695.

Increased demand for slaves, meanwhile, accentuated and refocused European interest in West Africa. However, trade there was not easy. For example, the Company of Adventurers of London Trading to the Ports of Africa (the Guinea Company), which was granted a monopoly by James I of England in 1618, only traded to the Gambia in 1618–21 before abandoning the unprofitable trade. A Scottish Guinea Company, which operated on the Gold Coast, was founded in 1634, but the Company (which, in fact, was largely London-based) had only limited success.[17] The overthrow of Crown authority as a result of the English Civil War (1642–6) challenged the monopoly rights that rested on it, and the Guinea Company lost its monopoly of the trade on the Gold Coast. Factories were established on that coast at Anomabu (1639) and Takoradi (1645), and interloping merchants came to be active; another factory was founded on the Benin coast.

There were also struggles over control of trade from West Africa, a prize made profitable in particular (though not exclusively) by the slave trade. In 1658, the Danish Crown provided backing for the seizure of the Swedish bases in West Africa, including the Swedish fort there, which was then sold to the Dutch West Africa Company. In 1661–4, there was a bitter conflict between the (British) Company of Royal Adventurers Trading into Africa, chartered in 1660, and the Dutch West Africa Company. In early 1661, the English Company sent out a small expedition using royal vessels under the command of the aggressive Captain Robert Holmes, a protégé of James, Duke of York, the Lord High Admiral. Holmes seized two islands in the mouth of the Gambia and attacked nearby Dutch forts, but the Dutch reacted sharply, seizing English ships and, in June 1663, capturing the English base at Cape Coast Castle. In November 1663, Holmes was sent to support the Company and uphold the rights of English subjects by force, and in early 1664 he seized the major Dutch settlements on the Gold Coast. However, a Dutch fleet under de Ruyter then recaptured these African settlements.[18] Such shifts in control greatly affected the local élites who were dependent on the trade.

The Anglo-Dutch Wars, which were formally from 1652 to 1654, 1665 to 1667, and 1672 to 1674, left Britain with a stronger position in West Africa. Its new bases included Cape Coast Castle (1652), Tasso Island (1663), Fort James (1664), and Accra, Apollonia, Elmina (the onetime Portuguese base of São Jorge da Mina), Winneba and Whydah (1672).

The foundation of bases reflected changing opportunities on the African coast. In the late seventeenth century there was a rise in the relative importance of slaves from sources north of the Equator, as opposed to Angola. In large part, this was a reflection of the greater *relative* significance of the West Indies as a market (as opposed to Brazil), although both Angola and Brazil remained crucial to the Atlantic slave trade. The Bight of Benin, where Anecho became a Portuguese base in 1645 and Whydah an English one in 1672, was of particular importance. By the end of the century, this area had extended to the Gold Coast. In contrast, the Bight of Biafra and the Sierra Leone coast did not become significant as major sources of slaves until the mid-eighteenth century.

The prospects offered by the slave trade encouraged many merchants – and numerous rulers – to enter it. At the beginning of the seventeenth century, Spanish pressure had helped deter Tuscany from persisting with plans to create colonies in Sierra Leone and Brazil, and the Duchy of Courland was unable to persevere with its plans; but Denmark, Sweden and Brandenburg-Prussia all established bases in West Africa, although the Swedes had lost all of theirs by the end of the 1650s.

Greater European demand for plantation goods led to an increase in the number of slaves imported into the Americas in the seventeenth century (an increase both over the previous century, and during the century itself). About half a million slaves were imported in the first half of the century, rising to a million in the second half, including over 600,000 in the last quarter.[19] The slave trade had initially been dominated by the need to supply the Portuguese and Spanish colonies with labour; however, as the Dutch, French and English expanded their colonial presence, they played a more direct role in the trade, selling to their own colonies, rather than simply to the Portuguese and Spanish colonies, as hitherto. The first slaving voyage from Bordeaux, which was to become a major base for the slaving trade, was made in 1672, although the French slave trade only really became important after 1713.

The English Company, which was reformed as the Royal African Company in 1672, was, by its charter, granted monopoly rights over the English slave trade between Africa and the West Indies. However, the undermining of the Company's position after the overthrow of the Stuarts in the Glorious Revolution of 1688–9 hit its finances and resulted in a decline both in government support and in the assertiveness of the Company. This led, in 1698, to the Company licensing private traders, as a key policy, in return for a ten per cent tax – its monopoly had become more unpopular due to its failure to meet the rising demand for slaves in the New World. This freeing of the African trade in 1698 legalized the position of those interlopers who became private traders, although some preferred to continue as interlopers. The Company was superseded by private traders, and the role thereby granted to private enterprise helped propel England to the fore in slave shipments.[20] In France, much of the seventeenth-century trade was by interlopers, and was thus clandestine, but the wars with the Dutch in 1672–8, and with the English and Dutch in 1689–97 and 1702–13, hit French trade hard.[21]

Higher death rates in the West Indies than in North America, and higher death rates for whites than for slaves, ensured that the colonies there did not become settler societies with large, locally born white populations. Yellow fever, which first struck in 1694, was to be a particular scourge that was especially virulent among whites previously unexposed to the disease, while malaria was also a serious problem. In part, disease was due to the slave trade itself, as the ships that brought the slaves also carried the mosquitoes that had the yellow fever virus, while the cutting down of forests for sugar hit the birds that preyed on the mosquitoes. Moreover, the clay pots used for sugar refining, once discarded and filled with rainwater, became breeding grounds for mosquitoes, which also fed off the sugar. The greater ability of blacks to adapt to the American tropics, and particularly their stronger resistance to yellow fever,[22] was seen by Europeans as justification for their use in hard labour, not least because, it was argued, this adaptation reflected the extent to which they were like animals.[23]

In North America, the British established their first permanent colony at Jamestown on the Chesapeake in 1607. The colony expanded as a result of the continued arrival of new settlers, and tobacco became the major crop in both Virginia and Maryland. The long terms of service exacted in return for transportation to Virginia and 'the extreme demand for labor' encouraged dealing in servants, and the hiring of servants was harsher and more degrading than in England.[24] Tobacco's limited capital requirements and high profitability encouraged settlers and investment; and, because it was an export crop, the links with England were underlined. The needs and difficulties of tobacco cultivation and trade, however, created serious problems for farmers, and this ensured particular sensitivity to labour availability and cost. Prior to the 1680s, savings in the costs of production and marketing were important in expanding the market. Then there were about three decades of stagnation at a time of rising labour prices, followed, during the eighteenth century, by increased demand, albeit also with rising production costs. Moreover, to complicate the general pattern, booms and busts created serious problems for producers. Alongside this, there was a shifting regional pattern in production.[25]

There was a move to slaves in the Chesapeake labour system in the decades around 1700. White indentured workers were difficult to retain in the face of the opportunities offered by rapidly spreading English settlement. As so often in the history of the slave trade, demographics proved a key element, in this case the fall in the birth rate in England in the 1640s. This hit Chesapeake planters in the early 1660s, with both fewer young men entering the Virginian labour market from England and a rise in real wages in Virginia.[26] These difficulties encouraged the move toward slaves.

An alternative labour source, that of the Native Americans, was hit by European diseases. Furthermore, the Native Americans resisted control, for instance on Grenada, St Vincent and across North America. Captured Native Americans were used as slaves (some being sent from Connecticut to Barbados after King Philip's War in 1675–6) and Tuscaroras defeated in Carolina in 1715 were enslaved; but their numbers were inadequate. African workers were also regarded as more effective and industrious than the Native Americans, and they commanded higher prices. This was true not only in Brazil, but also in eighteenth-century Carolina, and more generally. The profitability of the plantation economy made it possible – indeed desirable – to invest in these African workers.

In contrast to whites and Native Americans, slaves proved a more controllable labour force.[27] However, this was not always the case, as slave resistance developed, especially among escaped slaves on Jamaica.[28] Escapees often fled to the margins of settlement, such as the Dismal Swamp in North Carolina, where they were also an important aspect of relations between black and Native Americans.[29]

The development of slavery interacted with white racism. In Virginia, economic advantage and coercive power were linked to a belief that Africans were inherently inferior – an attitude that drew on what was seen as 'their God-given characteristics and the circumstances of their arrival in America'.[30] The establishment of Carolina as a separate colony in 1663 helped expand the English presence and also led to a rise in the slave economy of the English Atlantic. The new colony was closely linked to the English West Indies, providing opportunities for younger sons from the crowded islands, particularly Barbados. The settlers from these islands brought black slaves with them, ensuring that a sizeable black labour force soon developed in the new colony.[31] Carolina became a key exporter of colonial goods, including, from the 1690s, rice; the cultivation of both rice and indigo required large numbers of slaves.[32] Nevertheless, by 1700, only 23,000 Africans had arrived in English North America, and most of the labour needs were met by white servants. The crossing distance (and therefore time) to North America, a key index of profitability, was also greater than that from Africa to Brazil.

More generally, the price for male slaves was greater than that for females, both on the African coast and in the New World, and more males than females were imported into the latter, reflecting the role of demand factors in the trade, specifically the hard physical nature of the work that was expected. The profits and possibilities offered by slavery and the slave trade readily explain both, but it would be wrong to present the complex dynamics of enslavement simply in terms of rising demand for labour in the New World. It is also necessary to look at the African dimension. Accounts focusing on Western economic domination in Africa, on the way in which the Atlantic slave trade encouraged slavery within Africa, and on the gun–slave cycle (by which slaves were obtained by the Europeans in return for the provision of European guns to the Africans) are inadequate.[33] In large part this is because it was not until after the Industrial Revolution had transformed Western Europe's economy in the nineteenth century that traders could exert significant economic pressure on Africans, while European weapon sales, although important, do not provide the key to the trade.

Instead, it is necessary to focus on the supply of African labour, as well as the means of satisfying European demand, and also to offer a specific examination of the different slave-supplying regions in order to suggest the danger of broad generalizations. This is made more complex by the widening impact of Europeans along the African Atlantic coast, although the Bight of Biafra, to the east of the Niger delta, was not to become an important zone until the eighteenth century. What emerges clearly is a politics of frequent conflict within Africa that produced slaves, and of the rise and fall of empires, including the collapse of the Mali empire in about 1660. Fighting was also often linked to serious droughts and famine, although the introduction of maize, manioc and peanuts from the Americas helped population numbers. The seizure of people for slavery was seen as a way of weakening rivals; this was certainly the case in Senegambia and on the

Gold Coast. The availability of large numbers of slaves helped depress their price, which meant that their purchase was more efficient as a way of addressing economic needs in the New World. The relative inefficiency of African agriculture, particularly of cultivation (with its emphasis on the hoe), lowered the added value gained through African labour. This depressed the price of slaves and, in turn, encouraged their purchase.[34]

There have been serious difficulties in conceptualizing sub-Saharan statehood, and this contributes to the problem of how best to understand conflict there. There are problems in determining the nature of sovereignty and whether boundaries as currently understood existed at all. This difficulty has led to the frequent practice of using floating names on African maps. Many of the more durable conventions derived from the work of John Fage, who began with the contention that African sovereignty was vaguely defined and had a tendency to fade: strong at the centre, near the capital, and weaker toward the peripheries. Furthermore, he argued that, as African states ruled over people rather than over land, so the concept of a territorial boundary was not important. As a result, Fage opted for 'bubble' and circle maps, where a circle would be drawn with its centre on the capital and its radius a rough estimate of the extent of the power. 'Bubbles' were a product of circles, with allowances made for other circles or for geographical features that clearly hindered control.[35]

This approach was challenged by John Thornton, who argued that the African concepts of boundary were similar to those of early-modern Europe (although certainly not to those of the modern world). He presented the basic unit of African politics as a fairly small, discrete and well-bounded entity, which he termed the 'mini-state'. As African law did not recognize landed private property, and states did not assess land taxes, state jurisdiction became critically important in defining who was taxable and who not. Jurisdiction was ultimately territorially bounded, so that subjects of states could, and often did, cross the borders to escape taxation, though usually this only put them within the taxable boundaries of another similar state. Territorial boundaries encouraged the treatment of others as outsiders who could be enslaved.

For modern scholars, there are major problems in understanding the relations between the African polities; problems that may help explain the frequency of conflict between them in this period. The essential mapping problem lay with the larger units, which typically agglomerated mini-states, either by charging them tribute or by interfering in their institutional, judicial or leadership functions. This creates an impression of instability that may well have been reflected in violence. The point at which such a mini-state lost sovereignty and became part of a larger unit is problematic: was it when one recognized the supremacy of another with nominal presents, or when significant tribute was assessed, or when judicial functions or leadership positions were taken over and appointed from outside, or when boundaries were completely redrawn? Campaigning was a key aspect of the way in which states pursued their interests and redefined relations.[36]

Warfare between African powers certainly provided large numbers of slaves. European powers, in contrast, were not able to seize large numbers. By far the most expansionist European power in Africa was Portugal, but its experience there revealed the major limitations of European land warfare in Africa. In South-East Africa, Portuguese attempts to operate from bases in Mozambique up the River Zambezi and to exploit the civil wars in Mutapa (modern Zimbabwe) were thwarted in the 1690s, with Changamire, the head of the Rozwi empire, driving the Portuguese from the plateau in 1693. In Angola, the Portuguese were effective only in combination with African soldiers. Unlike the nineteenth-century pattern of European-organized units filled with African recruits, the Portuguese in seventeenth-century Angola were all organized together into a single unit with its own command structure, while the Africans, either mercenaries, subject rulers, or allies, were separately organized in their own units with their own command structure. It was only at the level of the army as a whole that Portuguese officers had command, providing control for entire operations.

The Portuguese found the Africans well armed with well-worked iron weapons, as good in some ways as Portuguese steel weaponry, and certainly better than the Native wood and obsidian weapons of the New World. Both the slow rate of fire of Portuguese muskets and the openness of African fighting formations reduced the effectiveness of the Portuguese firearms; their inability to deploy anything larger than a small force of cavalry ensured that they could not counter this open order; while their cannon had little impact on African earthwork fortifications. As in North America, firearms diffused rapidly, and Africans possibly even had them in equal numbers as early as the 1620s; certainly quantities of them were reported in 1626–8 in the first war against the formidable Queen Njinga of the Ndongo, who challenged the Portuguese position in Angola. The Portuguese victory over the shield-bearing heavy infantry of the kingdom of Kongo at the battle of Mbumbi (1622) was the result of overwhelming numerical superiority, not weapons superiority, and the Portuguese army withdrew very quickly and even returned captured slaves when the main Kongolese army reached the region. When they were left without African light infantry, Portuguese forces could well be destroyed, as by the forces of Queen Njinga at the battle of Ngolomene (1644).

   In contrast, the combination of Africans and European infantry, with its body armour and swordsmanship as well as firepower, was effective, as in the Portuguese victories over Njinga at Cavanga (1646) and over Antonio I of Kongo at Ambuila (1665). As a reminder that Europeans enjoyed no monopoly on firearms, Antonio's army included a small force of musketeers, as well as two cannon.

   The Portuguese victory at Ambuila has attracted some attention, but Kongo did not collapse rapidly. The Portuguese attempt to intervene in the Kongolese civil war led to a disastrous defeat at Kitombo (1670). This caused all hope of intervening in Kongo, even when it was severely divided in civil war, to be put aside. Kitombo showed that there was little to be gained even against a weaker Kongo.

In addition, a long series of wars against the kingdom of Ndongo that had begun in 1579 ended in stalemate for the Portuguese in the 1680s. After they took Pungo Andongo in a difficult siege in 1672 (and at considerable cost), the policy of the Portuguese in the African interior shifted away from large-scale wars aimed at conquest, and central Angola was not to be conquered by Portugal until the late nineteenth century.[37] Portugal would have found it difficult to carry war much further east against any sort of organized and determined resistance because of the need for extended supply lines. The same was true of the north (into Kongo), and the period of quiescence from the 1680s in part reflected acceptance of the fact.

Portuguese weakness in Africa, together with the contrasting strength of rival, non-Western slave traders, was demonstrated in East Africa. Fort Jesus, the mighty Portuguese garrison in Mombasa, fell in 1631 to a surprise storming by Sultan Muhammad Yusuf of Mombasa, and an expedition by the Portuguese from their major Indian base of Goa failed to regain it in 1632. The Portuguese were able to return when the Sultan abandoned the fortress under the pressure of Portuguese attack, but in 1698 it fell again, after a lengthy siege, to the Omani Arabs. The Portuguese presence north of Mozambique was thus lost, and a European territorial presence on the Swahili coast did not resume until the 1880s, when Germany and Britain established bases there.

The development of new military forms and the spread of firearms in West Africa also affected Western options, and need to be discussed in any treatment of the slave trade – not merely because they did have an impact on those options, but also because they influenced the pattern of slave availability. African warfare was transformed by the increasing preponderance of firepower over hand-to-hand combat, and by a growing use of larger armies. In West Africa, prior to the use of firearms, armies fought in close order, with javelin-men in the front line and archers behind, providing overhead fire. The javelins could be thrown or used as pikes, and the javelin-men were also equipped with swords, so that they were able to fight as individuals in 'open' order. Shock warfare prevailed. Lacking shields, the archers were essentially support troops, and the bow lacked the prestige of the javelin and sword.

From the mid-seventeenth century on, however, the role of archers increased in Akwamu and Denkyira, inland states of West Africa, and, as firepower became more important, this led to a more open formation and a wider battle frontage, with archers in the front line flanking the javelin-men. Thus, missile tactics came to prevail in West Africa even before the widespread use of firearms. The new military methods spread, for example, to Asante in the 1670s. Javelin-men came to play a tactical role subordinate to that of the bowmen, and between the 1660s and the 1690s the javelin was discarded as a weapon, becoming (like the halberd in Europe) essentially ceremonial.

In turn, the bow came to be supplanted by the musket. Firearms came into use in Africa over a long time span, in part because usage was restricted by the limited availability of shot and powder. The use of firearms in West Africa was first reported in Kano in the fifteenth century. Kano was one of the Islamic Hausa city-states that traded across the Sahara, but a regular force of musketeers was not organized there until the 1770s. On the West African coast, the Asebu army of the 1620s was the first to include a corps of musketeers, their guns being supplied by the Dutch, and muskets replaced bows in the 1650s to 1670s. However, the tactical shift towards open-order fighting did not come until later: musketeers were used as a shield for the javelin-men, and tactics centred on missile warfare were slow to develop in the coastal armies. Firepower, though, did increase in the 1680s and 1690s, as flintlock muskets replaced matchlocks, but bayonets were not used. In the forest interior of West Africa, muskets replaced bows in the 1690s and 1700s.

The emphasis on missile weapons, bows and, later, muskets interacted with socio-economic changes, and in particular with the transformation of peasants into militarily effective soldiers. This development led to the formation of mass armies and to wars that lasted longer. Larger armies increased the numbers that could be captured in conflicts, which took place over much wider areas and which could yield large numbers of slaves. Warfare based on shock tactics had been selective in its manpower requirements, but in Akwamu and Denkyira all males fit to bear arms were eligible for conscription. On the Gold Coast (coastal modern Ghana) and the Slave Coast (coastal modern Togo and Benin, formerly Dahomey), the replacement of shock by missile tactics was linked to a shift from élite forces relying on individual prowess to larger units, although in Dahomey there was an emphasis on a small standing army. These military changes were related to the rise of the states of Akwamu and Asante on the Gold Coast and Dahomey on the Slave Coast, and perhaps to the late seventeenth-century expansion of Oyo further east. These powerful states were to have a very great impact on European options, at a time of major expansion of the slave trade.

Unlike Portugal, other European powers did not try to make conquests in Africa, and the European presence in West Africa was anchored by coastal forts that served as protected bases for trade, although in some areas there were no settlements and the traders operated from their ships. These bases were vulnerable: the Dutch position at Offra and the French one at Glehue were destroyed in 1692; the Danish base at Christiansborg fell in 1693; and the secondary British base at Sekondi succumbed in 1694. In contrast, the leading British base at Cape Coast Castle, the overseas headquarters of the Royal African Company, which was gained in 1652, was never taken, and was successfully defended against African attack in 1688. Nevertheless, the British were well aware of the weakness of their position. The garrisons of European forts were indeed very small and relied upon the forces of African allies both for their own security and for their capacity to intervene in local conflicts.[38]

The emphasis was on co-operating with African rulers. British posts in West Africa were not held by sovereign right, but by agreement with local rulers – rent or tribute was paid for several posts, and the officials of the Royal African

Company sought to maintain a beneficial relationship with numerous local *caboceers* (leaders) and *penyins* (elders) through an elaborate and costly system of presents and jobs. On the Gold Coast, the Swedish African Company was able to play a role in the 1650s because the Futu élite wanted to balance the influence of the Dutch West India Company. Their co-operation was crucial to the establishment of new trading posts. Co-operation was a matter not only of trade but also of military and political support.[39]

Insofar as comparisons can be made, European slave traders did not enjoy coercive advantages in Africa any greater than those of their Arab counterparts on the Indian Ocean coast of Africa; while those of Moroccan and other slave raiders operating across the Sahara, and from the *sahel* belt into the forested regions further south, were probably superior. The major European advantage rested on purchasing power, and this derived from the prosperity of plantation economies in the Americas, and thus on the integrated nature of the Atlantic economy. But the Europeans did not have a monopoly of purchasing power. If the emphasis is on purchasing power, then a key element in the slave trade was not only the conflicts within Africa that produced slaves, but also the patterns of credit and debt that transmitted this purchasing power, opening African society to demands for labour. In this approach, the undercapitalized nature of the African economy emerges as important in creating a reliance on European credit, with the same being true for other external sources of credit in the shape of Arab slave traders.

Local co-operation in the slave trade was crucial.[40] Indeed, slavery entailed the interaction of the Western economic order and the dynamics of African warfare, with the victims of the latter caught in the middle.[41] The demands of the European-dominated Atlantic economy pressed on local African power systems and, in providing slaves, these systems served the Atlantic economy, while many slaves were kept for use in the local economy. African rulers proved more than willing to sell captives, and derived considerable profit from the trade. Indeed, the widespread belief among many Africans exported as slaves, that they had been sold to cannibals to be cooked and eaten, possibly expressed a wider opposition to the cannibalistic social politics of selling slaves to foreigners. Similarly, in African attitudes, there was a linkage of the trade to disease and to death – quite reasonably so. If the 'demand' side of the slave trade was morally reprehensible, so, too, was the 'supply' side.

The compromises entailed in interests that were shared through negotiations, and in the relations summarized as globalization, were thus made at the expense of others. It is important to see both the co-operation and the suffering. To treat the subject in terms only of compromise, or simply of coercion, is naïve and limited. Two popular religious movements in West Africa, led by Nasr al-Din in 1673–7 and Abd al-Kadir from 1776, counted hostility to the sale of slaves to Christians among their Islamic reform policies.[42] They failed, but they are a reminder of the contentious nature of the trade in contemporary Africa.

At the individual level, the reality of slavery was of the trauma of capture by African chieftains, sale to European merchants (often after passing through African networks), and transportation: violence, shock, hardship and disruption. Individuals were taken from their families and communities. Many died in the process of capture, although this is very obscure. Others died in the drive to the coast, in which they were force-marched, and joined by coffles, which secured them by the neck while leaving their legs free for walking. Again death rates during this stage are very obscure. Yet more died in the port towns, where they were crowded together in horrible, unhealthy conditions while awaiting shipment. At Cape Coast Castle, the slaves were confined in the vaulted brick slave hole, a twilight existence in which they were chained up round the clock, apart from when they were driven to the Atlantic coast twice daily in order to be washed. Others died on the ships that transported them across the Atlantic (the stage for which death rates have been calculated) or soon after arrival, as they were exposed to unaccustomed levels and types of disease. In the process of capture, transportation and sale, the slaves were also intimidated, humiliated and exposed to terrifyingly unfamiliar circumstances.

There are no precise figures for overall deaths, but certainly many slaves died on the Atlantic crossing, during which they were crowded together and held in poor, especially unsanitary, conditions, with holds proving both foetid and crowded. Furthermore, the slaves had already been weakened by their generally long journey to the Atlantic coast, and there was an unwillingness on the part of their captors to spend much on provisions. This exacerbated the health problems already caused by the impact of malnutrition, disease and conflict among those who had become enslaved. As a result, the slaves were more vulnerable on their journeys. Most died from gastro-intestinal illnesses, such as dysentery – a reflection of the very crowded nature of the ships and the dirty conditions in the holds. The percentage of deaths on a crossing clearly varied; if there was a delay, the casualty rates rose. But in any case, the rate was grim: it has been calculated that the average loss on Dutch ships between 1637 and 1645 was 17.9 per cent, and the losses for the British Royal African Company between 1680 and 1688 were about 23.5 per cent.[43] It is bare statistics that must record these experiences of brutal custody, for most of those involved are nameless.

This was only part of the wider process of loss to which the organization of the slave trade contributed, and the terrible nature of the Middle Passage across the Atlantic should not distract from the cruelties of the opening phases of the trade in Africa. More generally, as Joseph Miller has pointed out, under

> limitations on the technology of administration, transportation, and communications, sequential ownership may have represented efficient commercial organization from the point of view of the consumers of slave labour; but the passage of the slaves through the hands of numerous small specialists in Brazil and Angola meant that none of the slaves' successive owners

incurred responsibility for their long-term welfare ... each ... tried to maintain them in a physical condition minimally sufficient to allow quick resale.[44]

Albeit distantly, such treatment can be related to the powerful racism of the period, with its notion of a clear racial hierarchy. This was linked to false explanations, such as that of Marcello Malpighi (1628–94), professor of medicine in Bologna and the founder of microscopic anatomy, who believed that all men were originally white, but that the sinners had become black.

Once arrived in the Americas, the slaves were exposed to fresh difficulties and renewed humiliation and intimidation. Becoming habituated to new living and working environments in the so-called 'seasoning period' was difficult and led to a continuation of high death rates. These were accentuated by the conditions of work and life. Rates of seventy deaths per thousand were to be found on Barbados and Jamaica.[45]

Furthermore, many slaves were moved considerable distances once in the Americas. Large numbers were transported from entrepôts, such as Curaçao and Jamaica, to eventual mainland destinations. This involved fresh voyages, and also frequently-long marches overland. The former again exposed the slaves to overcrowding and the hazards this entailed, while the latter led to major problems, as new eco-systems were confronted. Furthermore, it was frequently necessary to wade rivers or to climb to considerable altitudes.

However, once transported, the Africans used their culture to adapt to the Americas, developing social and cultural practices that variously reflected African and hybrid forms.[46] The condition of slaves and former slaves was not simply that of oppression and labour. Urban slaves in Spanish America had, for example, reasonable opportunities to improve their position, and freedom was granted there with some readiness – far more so than in British or French America.[47] Slaves and former slaves also had a varied associational and cultural life with black and mulatto brotherhoods, for example in Brazil, which provided a range of social benefits for members. These brotherhoods responded in their make-up to the very varied nature of Brazilian black and mulatto society, and also demonstrated the capacity of this society to create its own hierarchies. Procedures included the election of governing bodies.[48] This was part of the process by which migration, however coerced, was a dynamic in which the whites who wielded political and economic power did not, or were unable to, prevent the development of independent associational patterns, a key stage in the creation of Black America.

CHAPTER 3

THE EIGHTEENTH CENTURY

In his novel *L'An 2440* (1770), the radical French writer Louis-Sébastien Mercier describes a monument in Paris depicting a black man, his arms extended, rather than in chains, and a proud look in his eye, surrounded by the pieces of twenty broken sceptres. He stands atop a pedestal bearing the inscription, 'Au vengeur du nouveau monde' ('To the avenger of the New World'). To his readers, this would have seemed a utopian prospect, and also proof of Mercier's radicalism. Though this was before the advent of photography, books no doubt brought home at least part of the nature of slavery to their European readers. In his far more successful novel *Candide* (1759), the leading French writer of the Enlightenment, Voltaire, has his protagonist visit Surinam (on the Atlantic coast of South America), which had been colonized by the Dutch as a plantation economy. A Negro tells Candide:

> Those of us who work in the factories and happen to catch a finger in the grindstone have a hand chopped off; if we try to escape, they cut off one leg. Both accidents happened to me. That's the price of your eating sugar in Europe ... Dogs, monkeys, and parrots are much less miserable than we are. The Dutch ... who converted me, tell me every Sunday that we are all children of Adam.[1]

The final sentence is a reference to Christian hypocrisy directed at the Calvinist Dutch. This point was to be echoed in 2003 when, on a visit to Africa, US President George W. Bush travelled to the major West African slave-trading post at Gorée, which had been used by Holland, France and Britain, and which is now in Senegal. This was a choice of destination designed to send a message about his concern for African-Americans, as well as his awareness of their distinctive history, and his grasp of the role of suffering in it. Bush declared that 'Christian men and women became blind to the clearest commands of their faith ... Enslaved Africans discovered a suffering Saviour and found him as more like themselves than their masters.'

Gorée and other ports were, indeed, very busy in the eighteenth century. It was the peak period of the slave trade, with about 52 per cent of those shipped from Africa to the Americas in the period 1450–1900 moved in that century alone.[2] There was a clear sense of the trade becoming larger in scale, more sophisticated and greater in importance. As before, the trade involved selling slaves to the colonies of other powers, and also to one's own colonies. Most obviously, both France and Britain sought to profit from demand in Latin America, and from the wealth of its economies.

In doing so, they contributed greatly to the illicit slave flows[3] that challenge the quantification of the slave trade, on which so much excellent work has been done. Nevertheless, in order to avoid the problems posed by the Spanish regulatory regime, which covered so much of the Americas from the Spanish colony of Florida southwards, it was far more desirable to gain permission to trade. Indeed, in 1701, as a sign of closer Franco-Spanish relations following the accession of the Bourbon Philip V to the Spanish throne the previous year, the French Guinea Company was granted the *asiento* contract to transport slaves to Spanish America for ten years, a lucrative opening into the protected trade of the Spanish empire.

In turn, the victorious British gained the right to trade with Spanish America in 1713, at the close of the War of the Spanish Succession (1702–13), a conflict in which they had defeated the French.[4] This right was exercised by the South Sea Company, and the extravagant hopes it gave rise to helped launch the vast speculative bubble in shares in the Company that famously burst in 1720, creating a major political scandal over governmental connivance in fraudulent practices. The role of the South Sea Company also created tensions in the British slave trade, with, for example, the Royal African Company pressing the ministry for assistance against the Company in 1724.

Unlike Britain and France, powers that lacked important colonies were dependent on selling to others. The Dutch had bases on the Gold Coast of West Africa, including Axim, Hollandia, Accadia, Butri and Shama, but in the Americas they lacked a market comparable to Portuguese Brazil, French Saint-Domingue (modern Haiti), or British Jamaica. Instead, they sold to all they could reach through entrepôts on their West Indian islands of Curaçao and St Eustatius, and carried about 310,000 slaves in the course of the century.[5] Centred on Cape Town, which had been founded in 1652 as a base on the way to the Indian Ocean, Cape Colony was another Dutch slave society.[6]

In a weaker position, the Brandenburg (Prussian) and Danish companies were unable to make money this way. Indeed, in 1717, the two forts that the Brandenburg Company had on the Gold Coast, Fort Dorothea (Accadia) and Fort Friedrichsburg (Hollandia), were sold to the Dutch.

Three Danish West Indian companies in succession failed to make the necessary profits: the Danes owned several small islands in the West Indies – St Croix, St John and St Thomas (sold in 1917 to the USA, and now the American Virgin Islands) – but lacked a large market. The Danes transported just over 50,000 slaves from Africa between 1733 and 1802, and about 74,000 during the century as a whole.[7] The Danish colonial presence on the African Gold Coast had begun in the 1650s, with Christiansborg acquired from Sweden in 1653, and Fort Augustenborg in 1700. The motives of the government, which supported the companies involved financially and with monopoly rights and other privileges, were mercantilist and cameralist. In the first case, the intention was that Denmark should obtain part of the wealth created by the international slave trade, in order to strengthen Danish commercial groups (and thus the country) financially. In a narrower sense, there was also a drive to gain larger revenues for the Treasury. Thus, entry into the slave trade can be seen as an aspect of a more general government policy that was intended to further trade and industry and strengthen the state.

The Danish role in the slave trade really started in the eighteenth century. So, after the short-lived attempt in the mid-seventeenth century, did that of Sweden, which gained the island of St Barthélemy from France in 1784; it was returned in 1877. In exchange for being ceded the island, Gustavus III of Sweden had granted his ally, France, a depot for naval stores at Göteborg (Gothenburg). Gustavus had notions of colonies in Africa, but the person he sent out to gather information, Carl Bernhard Wadström, instead became a rather prominent abolitionist.

More generally, the slave trade was not a constant. Flows varied, as the sources and destinations of slaves changed. The majority of Africans transported in the eighteenth century went to the West Indies and Brazil, with less than a fifth going to Spanish and North America.[8] The biggest shippers were Britain, Portugal, France and the United Provinces (Dutch Republic, Modern Netherlands), in that order. Anglophone scholarship concentrates heavily on Britain, but France was also a key supplier to the West Indies, and it is pertinent to note its role.

During the century, the French colonies obtained 1,015,000 slaves from French sources, but an illegal British trade was also important, and this makes it difficult to assess the total numbers imported into these colonies.[9] In 1788, the French West Indies contained 594,000 slaves, many of them harshly treated. In 1687, Saint-Domingue, the largest French colony in the West Indies (modern Haiti), contained 4,500 whites and 3,500 blacks; in 1789 there were 28,000 whites, 30,000 free blacks and 406,000 slaves. In the 1780s, thanks to strong re-exports, sugar prices rose, despite a general recession in France.[10] This was the peak decade for the French West

Indian colonies to receive slaves: nearly 30,000 annually. The numbers sent to Saint-Domingue rose from 14,000 annually in 1766–71 to 28,000 annually in 1785–9, and the strength of the colony's economy ensured that it was able to get a better choice of slaves. Large numbers of slaves were also sent to the French West Indian islands of Guadeloupe and Martinique. The French, having established their first base in Louisiana in 1699, imported the first slaves to the colony in 1719, although it never became a major slave society.[11]

The main French source of slaves was the basin of the River Senegal, via the slaving ports of Gorée and St Louis. In contrast, Assinie, on the Ivory Coast, was held by the French only from 1687 to 1705, and Forcados, on the Benin coast, was held only from 1786 to 1792. The French could be forceful in West Africa, as in 1724, when a naval force seized the Dutch base of Arguin on the coast of modern Mauritania, in an area where the French claimed exclusive commercial privileges. In a separate trade, slaves from East Africa and Madagascar supplied the French colonies in the Indian Ocean.[12] Réunion, which France had claimed in 1642, was a source of coffee, and Mauritius, seized in 1715, provided sugar. In 1769–72, French expeditions acquired clove plants on Ambon in the East Indies and introduced them to Mauritius.

As a result of the efforts of the slaves, exports from the Americas boomed, and this contributed to a major rise in European consumption: of coffee, from two million pounds at the start of the century to 120 million pounds at the end; of chocolate (from two million to 13 million pounds); and of tobacco, especially from Virginia (from 50 million to 125 million pounds). In each case, this was a rise that far outstripped the increase in the European population.[13] Between 1663 and 1775, imports of sugar for England and Wales rose from 8,176 tons to over 97,000 tons. In 1702, visiting the port of Falmouth, John Evelyn had 'a small bowl of punch made with Brazil sugar'. In September 1764, the merchant fleet from Pernambuco in North-East Brazil was reported as arriving in Lisbon with 5,000 chests of sugar.[14] Thanks to its plantation economy, Jamaica in the early 1770s was the wealthiest

British colony in the New World, and the average white there was 36.6 times as wealthy as the average white in the Thirteen Colonies.[15]

The French West Indian islands were particularly important for the production of sugar, and this helped drive forward French trade and production, interacting with opportunities in domestic and foreign markets. At the beginning of the century, Bordeaux's sugar refiners enjoyed the right to transport their product to much of France without having to pay many of the internal tolls of which their rivals in La Rochelle, Marseilles and Nantes complained. Bordeaux's imports of sugar, indigo and cacao from the French West Indies tripled in 1717–20 – the beginning of a massive increase in re-exports to northern Europe, which competed directly with those of Britain in key markets such as Hamburg. In 1778, Saint-Domingue exported 1,634,032 quintals of sugar (100 kilograms to a quintal).

Sugar was not alone. After the Caracas Company was founded in 1728 and given monopoly rights by the Spanish government to transport cacao from Venezuela, exports increased and the already established growth in production there continued. This encouraged the rise in slave imports: twice as many arrived in the region in the eighteenth century as in the seventeenth.[16]

The role of the New World continued strong because there was nowhere else that could produce significant quantities of its tropical goods. Whereas New England and North Carolina iron and timber goods had to compete on the British market with Scandinavian production, there was no equivalent competition for sugar. In 1792, the West Indies interest lobbied hard and successfully against an attempt by the British East India Company to export sugar from India, which might have led to a price cut.[17]

This interest was a powerful one, and it helped affirm the importance of the West Indies to the British political economy. The merchants trading with the West Indies lacked a company structure, but their pressure-group tactics and their ability to mount well-organized petitioning and propaganda campaigns were very important in persuading the Westminster Parliament, in which they were well represented, to pass a series of measures in their favour, such as the Molasses Act of 1733, and also to influence other legislation, such as the Sugar Act of 1764. This lobby became even more organized and active with the problems posed by the American Revolution.[18]

Coffee was another major product from the New World, and, thanks to slavery, the Europeans took over the bulk of the world trade in that commodity. In 1660, the leading French Mediterranean port of Marseilles imported only 19,000 quintals of Yemeni coffee (via Egypt – an important aspect of France's trade with the Ottoman Empire); by 1785 it was importing 143,310 quintals, of which 142,500 came from the West Indies. Introduced to Martinique and Guadeloupe in 1725, and to Saint-Domingue in 1730, French West Indian coffee was more popular than that produced by the Dutch in the East Indies, and it swiftly became the principal global source. From 1722, the French also produced coffee in Cayenne (French Guiana). In 1770, 350,000 quintals of coffee were produced by the French in the Americas, and in 1790 over 950,000. Most went to France, and much was then re-exported – from Marseilles, principally to the Ottoman empire, thus reversing the earlier trade flow. By 1789, Saint-Domingue was also probably supplying more than half the Western world's coffee. The Dutch began coffee production in Surinam in 1712, and by 1772 were producing over twelve million pounds per annum there,[19] which was part of the commercial rationale for the situation depicted in *Candide*.

The European presence in the East Indies was far more limited than in the West Indies, and was also more dependent on local co-operation. The Dutch East India Company introduced coffee into Java, and also imported pepper, sugar and indigo from there. Coffee production on Java quickly became considerable, while cloves, tea and coffee came from Ambon. However, due to political problems and distance, these trades could not match those from the West Indies, and the heavily regulated nature of the Dutch East India Company did not help – the Company wanted limited supplies at high prices, rather than massive quantities that could compete on world markets at low prices.

Leaving aside the most prominent goods, the provision of other New World products also depended on slaves. Thus, the British logwood cutters who settled in Belize in Central America brought in African slaves after 1720, and from the 1760s brought in even more to help with mahogany cutting, which required additional slaves.

Trade with the New World, in turn, affected much of the European economy. For example, although the colonial trade at Bordeaux was conducted by French merchants, re-exports were largely controlled by foreign firms established in the town. At the beginning of the century, most of these were Dutch, but by 1730 there was a significant German presence. Towards the end of the century, Milanese merchants brought coffee, chocolate, sugar and spices to Switzerland, purchasing the muslins of St Gallen and Zürich in return.

France's production of colonial goods and its slave trade were affected by war with Britain, and eventually, in the 1790s, by a major and ultimately successful slave rebellion on Saint-Domingue. This war with Britain, which broke out in 1792, was the last that century of a sequence of wars that involved conflict in West Africa and the Americas. These conflicts affected both the slave trade and the exports from the New World that it fed, although it was generally the case that disputes over competing interests in the West Indies and West Africa did not lead to sustained hostilities, let alone war. In 1739, Anglo-Spanish differences over trade in the Caribbean led to the War of Jenkins' Ear, but, in the eighteenth century, disputes in West Africa did not have such consequences.

Indeed, disputes were often with allies. The British Royal African Company frequently complained of attacks: in October 1723, the Portuguese destroyed its trading settlement at Cabinda, an example of the Portuguese determination to control the trade from the north of the River Congo; in 1725, the Company complained about French action on the Guinea coast; and in 1728, Dutch attacks upon its ships led to demands for naval protection and the dispatch of a British warship. The issue, however, did not arouse much domestic interest, and the same was true of Dutch–Portuguese rivalry over the slave trade from West Africa in the mid-1720s.

In the 1730s, tension in West Africa centred on Anglo-French competition, although this focused on the gum trade from the River Senegal, rather than on the slave trade. The French sought to limit the establishment of a British position on the River Gambia, while the British argued that French settlements on one part of the coast did not give the French a right to the trade along the whole coast.[20] Conflict was avoided because neither state sought to fight, and neither was under significant domestic pressure on the issue. The Royal African Company was unpopular in Britain, suffering as it did from the widespread dislike of the monopolistic position of chartered companies that was a characteristic of British public discussion of trade. In contrast, those merchants, politicians and commentators pressing for an assertive policy in the West Indies were able to identify themselves with a strong and expansionist image of the national interest.

Later in the century, there was also reluctance to push disagreements in West Africa, whether with allies or with rivals. In 1784, a memorandum about the French establishing a post on the River Gambia at once led to government enquiries in Britain, but again the response was subdued.[21] In 1791, there was concern over the position at Ambriz to the north of the Portuguese settlements on the Angolan coast but to the south of the River Congo. British trade was seen as threatened by Portuguese claims, but the issue was not pushed forcefully by Britain.[22]

Disputes over control of the sugar islands in the West Indies were more sensitive, although they did not lead to large-scale hostilities. British settlers were expelled from St Lucia by the French in 1723; although the episode created political difficulties for the British government, it did not become a major issue. Similarly, Anglo-Danish differences in 1733 over claims to the island of St Croix did not assume major importance.

In contrast, once war had begun, the sugar islands were a major site of conflict. This was less the case in the War of the Austrian Succession, in which the British captured Port Louis on Saint-Domingue in 1748. In the Seven Years' War (1756–63), by contrast, the British captured Guadeloupe in 1759, and Grenada, Martinique, St Lucia and St Vincent in 1762. The French slave stations in West Africa, St Louis and Gorée, were taken in 1758. Havana was captured from Spain in 1762. Under the 1763 peace settlement (the Peace of Paris), Martinique, Guadeloupe, Cuba, Gorée and St Lucia were returned, but Grenada, St Vincent and St Louis in Senegal were retained. John, 3rd Earl of Bute, George III's key adviser, had noted 'When Choiseul [the French foreign minister] gives Senegal up and seems facile on Gorée, it is with an express proviso that the French be put in possession of a sea port on the Slave Coast.'[23] After the war, the French mapped Martinique and Guadeloupe in order to provide information in the event of future hostilities with Britain. Mapping was carried out by engineers and was linked to a policy of fortification. The maps recorded the plantation system, and the names of the plantation owners were also marked.[24]

In the War of American Independence, Gorée changed hands in 1779, while, in the West Indies, the French also took Dominica (1778), Grenada (1779), St Vincent (1779), Tobago (1781), Nevis (1782), St Christopher (1782), and Montserrat (1782), although the British captured St Lucia (1778). The British slave trade was hit by the war, and the profitability of the sugar plantations suffered, too.[25] In the eventual peace settlement, the Treaty of Versailles (1783), conquests were returned, although France retained Tobago and Senegal. In the French Revolutionary War, which broke out in 1793, the slave trade and the plantation economies of the West Indies were disrupted anew. The British captured Gorée in 1800, and, in the West Indies, Tobago in 1793, St Lucia in 1794 and again in 1796 (it had been retaken in 1795), Trinidad in 1797, Surinam in 1799, Curaçao in 1800, and the Danish and Swedish West Indian islands in 1801.

In contrast, the Portuguese slave trade in the South Atlantic did not face any challenge comparable to that mounted by the Dutch the previous century in both Angola and Brazil. Angola, where the major bases were Luanda and Benguela, supplied about two million slaves during the eighteenth century, mostly to Brazil. The Portuguese had more bases further north, especially at Cacheu in Portuguese Guinea, and also traded along coasts where they did not have any bases. Off the Atlantic coast, they also had the islands of Annobon, Fernando Póo, Principe and São Tomé, although Annobon and Fernando Póo were gained by Spain in 1776. Otherwise, Spain had no direct presence in the African slaving world.

Growing demand for slaves in Brazil reflected its major economic expansion, but also the economic change taking place. The sugar plantations of the North-East declined in importance from the 1710s, as sugar production from the West Indies became more important in supplying European markets. This was an important aspect of the competition, and thus the search for comparative advantage, that the slave trade reflected. However, there was major growth in the South, where captaincies were founded for São Paulo (1709), Minas Gerais (1720), Goiás (1744) and Mato Grosso (1748). Furthermore, gold and diamond extraction from the Brazilian province of Minas Gerais, where gold had been discovered in 1695, grew substantially in significance.[26] This produced a key demand for slaves in a different area and was, simultaneously, a major new stimulus for the slave trade, helping as it did to fund the purchase of slaves. Slaves worked both in mines and at tasks such as washing diamond-bearing rocks. In March 1723, the arrival of the Rio de Janeiro fleet in Lisbon was reported, with 'considerable quantity of unregistered gold'.[27] Aside from Minas Gerais, where the towns of Minas Novas and Diamantina were founded in 1727 and 1730, respectively, there were gold deposits in Goiás and Mato Grosso. From the latter years of the century, in another important geographical shift, sugar and coffee plantations near Rio de Janeiro became prominent. In 1763, Rio de

Janeiro replaced Salvador (Bahia), further north, as the capital of Brazil.

There was considerable differentiation in the slave trade. The Portuguese bases in Angola supplied Minas Gerais and Rio de Janeiro with slaves, while West Africa supplied the sugar plantations of North-East Brazil,[28] and this differentiation was an aspect of the wider specialization of the Atlantic slave trade. It took about 40–45 days to sail from Elmina in West Africa to Salvador (Bahia), and about fifty days to sail from Luanda in Angola to Rio.[29] The partnership between Europeans and élite Africans was crucial to this trade, with Luso-African families, who spanned the Portuguese world of the Angolan coast and the African world of the interior, also having links to the plantation-owning families of North-East Brazil. Plantation goods exported from Brazil included sugar, tobacco, coffee and, from the 1760s, cotton.[30] By 1800, there were over one million slaves in Brazil.

Although the Brazilian plantations relied on African slave labour, and most slaves came from Angola, slave raiding was still practised in Brazil at the expense of Natives. Slave traders from São Paulo, known as Paulistas or *mamelucos*, did much to lower Native numbers, although they were resisted by the *reducciones*, Jesuit-supervised frontier settlements in Spanish America, where Natives grew crops. This encouraged the Portuguese to close down the Jesuit settlements. Native slaves and forced labour were important to Amazonia for the collection of cacao, sarsaparilla and other forest products. However, in 1743–9 possibly half the Native population of the Amazon valley fell victim to measles and smallpox.[31]

The growth in exports from Spanish America was also linked to the intensification of slavery, which encouraged the import of slaves. This was true of the export of sugar and tobacco from Cuba, cacao and sugar from Mexico, and cacao, tobacco, cotton, coffee, sugar and indigo from Venezuela, where, by 1800, about 15 per cent of the 800,000-strong population were slaves working in the plantations. The economic importance of slave production in South America is generally underrated, as the Anglophone literature focuses on the West Indies and on what became the USA.

At the same time, a point that undermines arguments based simply on racialism is that part of the black population of Latin America (as elsewhere) was not enslaved. Moreover, there was a willingness to arm the free blacks. From 1764, they were increasingly recruited into the militia in Spanish America. Furthermore, defence of the interior of the French colony of Cayenne was entrusted to Native Americans and free blacks, who were organized into a company of soldiers, while, in the 1760s and 1770s, black and mulatto Brazilians were recruited into companies of irregular infantry.[32] This was far less common in British America.

Brazil provided a market for British slave traders, and there were British and French sales (both legal and illegal) to Spanish America. However, for British and French merchants alike, the core trade consisted in selling slaves to their own colonies. The British were the most prominent in the slave trade. Between 1691 and 1779, British ships transported 2,141,900 slaves from African ports, and British colonial ships took a further 124,000.[33] London dominated the trade until the 1710s, when it was replaced by Bristol;[34] the developing port of Liverpool took the leading position from the 1740s. The regulatory framework that had maintained London's control had been dismantled in 1698, when the African trade was freed from the control of the Royal African Company. This legalized the position of private traders, and made shifts in the relative position of ports far easier.

The values of liberalization for increased trade were to be seen, on a different scale, with the removal of restrictions on the Mozambique trade from South-East Africa in the second half of the century. The monopoly role of companies was ended when Mozambique was removed from the jurisdiction of Portuguese India, and in 1786 the monopoly of the port of Mozambique was ended. Other ports in the colony gained their own customs houses and began trading. This led to an expansion in the slave trade from South-East Africa that was also related to the ability to expand the area in the interior from which slaves were obtained. This expansion rested on the purchase of slaves, not on the territorial expansion attempted earlier in the colony's history; that was not resumed until the late nineteenth century.

In Britain, the shift from Bristol to Liverpool as the leading slave port was readily apparent. In 1725, Bristol ships carried about 17,000 slaves and, between 1727 and 1769, 39 slavers were built there; by 1752, Liverpool had 88 slavers with a combined capacity of over 25,000 slaves. In 1750-79, there were about 1,909 slave-trade sailings from Liverpool, 869 from London, and 624 from Bristol.[35] Liverpool had better port facilities than Bristol, including the sole wet dock outside London, and there was a major expansion of dock facilities, with the opening of the Salthouse Dock (1753), St George's Dock (1771) and Duke's Dock (1773).

Most slaves were transported by the British to the West Indies, which were at the centre of the British slave economy, but many also went to British North America. The number of slaves there rose from about 20,000 in 1700 to over 300,000 by 1763, particularly as South Carolina and then, later, Georgia were developed as plantation economies, supplementing those on the Chesapeake. In South Carolina and, eventually, Georgia, rice became an additional plantation crop, reflecting the particular opportunities of the tidewater environment.

The slave trade was integral to the commercial economy and the shipping of the British Atlantic; was crucial to entrepreneurial circles in Britain, and to the financial world there; and exerted a range of influences elsewhere in Britain, particularly, but not exclusively, in the ports. Not only were the large ports of Liverpool, Bristol, Glasgow and London involved in the trade, but so also were smaller ports, such as Barnstaple, Bideford, Dartmouth, Exeter, Lancaster, Plymouth, Poole, Portsmouth, Topsham and Whitehaven. This last saw about 69 slaving voyages to Africa between 1710 and 1769, most after 1750, and its merchants were probably the fifth most important group of slave traders in Britain in the latter period.[36] The role of the smaller ports helped spread the impact of the slave trade on the British economy, although many, including Devon's ports, played only a minor role, and many merchants and ships were involved in the trade on only a temporary basis.

Returns from slave-trading ventures were risky, but were also sufficiently attractive to keep some existing investors in the trade and to entice new investors to join up; and the returns could enable men of marginal status to prosper sufficiently to enter the merchant class. Furthermore, the triangular pattern of Atlantic trade – goods, both British manufactures and imports (such as East India Company textiles), from Britain to Africa; slaves thence to the New World; and colonial products, such as sugar and tobacco, back to Britain[37] – was practicable for small-scale operators, as the outlay required was less than that needed for the trade to the more distant East Indies. The triangular trade depended on credit and the ability to wait for payment, and Britain's financial strength provided both. The role of finance, particularly of the sugar commission business, ensured that London, where the business was centred, was as heavily involved in the trade as Liverpool.[38] Financial buoyancy was particularly important in long-distance trade, in which new ships lasted only two or three voyages, financial returns were delayed, and merchants needed to obtain long-term credit on favourable terms.

The trade brought prosperity to British manufacturers. The export of goods to Africa as part of the triangular trade helped broaden the range of groups in British society who were interested in the slave trade and who benefited from its expansion. Africa was seen as a sphere of opportunity, not least because trade to much of the rest of the world appeared blocked or limited by the role of other European states, for example Spain, which was determined to limit trade with its colonies, as well as by the attitude of non-European powers, by the entrenched position of British chartered companies, such as the East India Company, and by the lack of any product worth obtaining in return for exports. The last, for example, limited Portuguese and Dutch interest in Australia. In his 'Thoughts on the African Trade', published in 1730 in number 76 of the *Universal Spectator*, 'J. L.' attacked the position of the British East India Company in trade to the Indian Ocean, and urged the establishment of a trade to the south-east coast of Africa, involving the export of textiles and pewter. This, he argued, would help British industry, whereas, he claimed, the trade to India brought no such advantages. The suggestion did not bear fruit, but was indicative of the sense of Africa as a land of opportunity for British trade. This argument was later to be taken up by abolitionists, who claimed that abolition of the slave trade would create major new opportunities for British exporters.

The triangular trade also offered considerable flexibility. For example, when sugar became harder to obtain from the West Indies, Lancaster's traders found other imports in which to invest their proceeds from slave sales, particularly mahogany, rum and dyewoods, each of which was in demand in Britain. This enabled them to maximize their profits on each leg of their enterprise, which was particularly important for marginal operators trading in a competitive field. When competition did eventually make the slave trade less viable at Lancaster, the contracts and experiences forged by the African trade ensured that other opportunities were available to merchants.[39]

As far as the profitability of French trade was concerned, La Rochelle's colonial trade was affected by the wild fluctuations in slave-trade profits, as well as by wars and attendant colonial losses. As a result, merchant families tended not to limit their business endeavours to maritime trade – nor to any single branch of such trade.[40] Nevertheless, long-distance trade was more profitable than private notarized credit, and was as profitable as government bonds (and safer).[41] Risk and solvency were also serious problems in the slave trade from Angola to Brazil, while difficulties in attracting investment affected the Coriso Company, established by Portugal in 1723 to export slaves to North-East Brazil. It collapsed in 1725.

The triangular trade was not the sole commercial system that was developed to help finance and exploit slavery. Supplying food and other products to the slave plantations was also important. Kendal was an English inland town that did not have close links to a major port; yet, in his *Tour of Scotland 1769* (1771), Thomas Pennant recorded how trade had encouraged local industry, which was chiefly

> engaged in manufactures of ... a coarse sort of woollen cloth called cottons sent to Glasgow, and from thence to Virginia for the use of the Negroes ... the manufactures employ great quantities of wool from Scotland and Durham.

Similarly, some of the expansion in French exports to the West Indies was for the growing population of the French West Indies, although much of the production was re-exported to the Spanish empire. In 1741–2, Bordeaux exported over eight million livres worth of produce to the French West Indian colonies annually, principally wine and textiles. The comparable figure for 1753–5 was over ten million.

There was also, as part of the British commercial world, the development of a trade in salt cod from Newfoundland, both to the West Indies and to Charleston, the port for South Carolina. Moreover, food was shipped from the Thirteen Colonies to the British West Indies. The colonial contribution included slaving from Rhode Island, from the ports of Newport, Bristol and Providence. Rhode Island lacked the agricultural opportunities offered elsewhere in the bigger colonies, but it produced rum that could be exported in return for slaves.[42] There were similar developments in other colonial systems.

Accumulated experience in the slave trade helped improve responsiveness to opportunities, lessen risk, and increase the efficiency of the trade – an efficiency that included a responsive African supply system.[43] It was possible to expand supply to meet changes in demand, and there was also a successful search for new sources of supply. The slave trade, nevertheless, involved serious commercial risks: a lack of sufficient slaves or, alternatively, the glutting of markets were issues that greatly affected profitability. The trade was expensive to enter, and the scale of the profits is unclear. While there is evidence of considerable profits, and of a resulting major contribution to investment and economic growth in Britain, there are more modest estimates, and even suggestions that, at the level of the individual voyage, the slave trade did not, by and large, bring great profits (if any). Concern about the profitability of the trade was a major factor in the pronounced variation in the number of voyages per year from individual ports. Larger firms had a considerable advantage.[44] Because the majority of British ships involved made only one voyage in the trade, there was no substantial separate slave fleet. Partly as a result of this, many slave ships were not the large ships that tend to attract attention, but smaller vessels carrying a limited number of slaves. Most fell within the 50–150 ton range.[45] Similarly, for the Portuguese trade, the large *galeras* were less important than the more modestly sized *bergantim*.

For Britain, as for other countries, the individual merchant and the individual voyage were a key factor.[46] However, the collapse of the Royal African Company meant that this was particularly true of the British trade. The Company's bases allowed it to exercise a function of sovereignty in a sphere where the state did not wish to get involved. However, this entailed a considerable financial and organizational burden. In 1730, the near-bankrupt Company petitioned for money to maintain its forts and settlements, and from 1730 to 1747 it received an annual subsidy from the government. The financial arrangement agreed in 1698 could not save the Company's poor finances, and, in 1750, it was abolished by the African Trade Act, which opened the trade to all subjects willing to pay a fee. With the help of a block grant from Parliament, the Company's bases were to be maintained by a successor company, the Company of Merchants Trading to Africa, which was controlled by the leading slave traders. The poor financial state of the Dutch West India Company, and the heavy cost of its West African operations, meant that it depended on government subsidies.

As an indication of the range of difficulties facing slave traders, Bristol merchants in the early 1730s were hit by shortages of slaves; by falling profits on colonial re-exports, as prices dropped; and by deteriorating relations with Spain, which created doubt about security and markets. War finally broke out in 1739, and the number of slave voyages from Bristol fell from 53 in 1738 to eight in 1744. The war only ended in 1748, and throughout, British merchants were heavily exposed to privateering. Whitehaven merchants largely abandoned the trade after 1769.

There was also rivalry between British commercial interests over the opportunities created by the Atlantic world. In 1739, for example, British merchants supported agitation for the export of sugar from Britain's West Indian colonies direct to European markets – a move resisted by the British sugar refiners. Pressure against Britain's entrepôt role was intended to reduce the cost of British colonial goods and to increase flexibility for merchants, but, as in this case, it also challenged British industrial interests involved in processing.

Aside from the uncertainty of the trade, profitability was also hit by the human cost of slavery, in the shape of the frequently (although not invariably) high death rate on the Atlantic crossing. If, with time, the proportion of deaths declined appreciably, this was largely thanks to shorter journey times, rather than to improved conditions, although a reduction in the crowding on ships was also important.[47] Slaver captains were less interested in slaves' survival than were the slave owners. In particular, there was little interest in costly medical care. Many of the officers and crew involved in the trade also died, in part as a consequence of their exposure to tropical diseases. In 1785–1807, 10–15 per cent of British captains died each year. Of the 940 men who made up the crews of 24 Bristol ships in 1787, 26 died during the voyage, and 239 deserted or were discharged in the colonies. With such casualties, it was scarcely surprising that the slave trade was very unpopular among sailors.[48]

Warfare in Africa among African powers continued to provide large numbers of slaves.[49] The intensive nature of warfare in much of the Atlantic hinterland – for example, the long civil war in Kongo[50] or the westward advance of the Lunda empire – fed the slave trade, as did droughts and famines. The *sahel* belt also saw widespread conflict. For example, the Pashalik of Timbuktu declined under pressure from the Tuareg and was destroyed by them in 1787. In its place, the Bambara people, whose principal town was Segu, extended their power down the River Niger. In the forest zone of West Africa, musketeers had largely replaced archers on the Gold Coast in the seventeenth century, and did so on the Slave Coast in the eighteenth. Asante in the former and Dahomey in the latter were expansionist powers whose conflicts produced slaves.[51]

Alongside this supply-side account, it is also pertinent to note the degree to which the slave trade helped transform society, hitting earlier patterns of hierarchy and identity, and savaging agrarian communities. Trends in slave prices suggest that the external demand factor became more important from mid-century and, as a result, that domestic forces became less important in the history of the regions affected.[52] For most of the century, nevertheless, variations in the productivity of the trade, not least the time spent by ships off Africa, reflected African forces – namely shifts in slave supplies within Africa. Indeed, British terms of trade with West Africa had fallen heavily in the 1720s and then again in the 1750s–70s, before rising in the 1780s and 1790s, although to a figure that was only about a third that of the 1700s. From the last quarter of the century, European advances in shipping and organization became important and helped ensure major gains in productivity.[53]

In West Africa, there was diffusion of European arms without political control, although the traffic in firearms developed more slowly away from the coast. Muskets, powder and shot were imported in increasing quantities, and were particularly important in the trade for slaves. For example, in the Senegal valley, gifts of guns were used to expand French influence. There is little evidence that Europeans provided real training in the use of firearms, although rulers did show a keen interest in seeing European troops and their local auxiliaries exercise in formation. The auxiliaries were crucial to the security of the European positions and to the offensive capability of European forces, and were probably the key figures in the transfer of expertise. Since they often performed seasonal work for the Europeans, and were trained to use firearms, for example in the riverboat convoys on the River Senegal, they had ample opportunity to sell their expertise to local rulers.

There is evidence that the troops of some African kingdoms trained in formation. Further, there are a few cases of Africans capturing European cannon and putting them to use, but field pieces were not normally sold to them, although some were given as gifts. West African blacksmiths could make copies of flintlock muskets, which replaced the matchlock as the principal firearm export to the Gold and Slave Coasts from about 1690; but casting cannon was probably beyond their capability.[54]

African firearms were not up to European standards, but they served their purpose and they became the general missile weapon over much of Africa, for example in Angola and on the Gold and Slave Coasts. The kingdom of Dahomey under King Agaja (*c.* 1716–40) in part owed its rise to an effective use of European firearms, combined with standards of training and discipline that impressed European observers; weaponry alone was not enough. Europeans on the Slave Coast had to take careful note of Dahomey views, and they had to make sure their quarrels did not disrupt that kingdom. Two French officers provided the Dahomians with military guidance in the 1720s, including instruction on how to dig trenches.[55] Dahomey supplied the slaves exported from the Bight of Benin.

An emphasis on firearms puts the Europeans centre-stage, but the role of firearms should not be exaggerated. The Mahi, whose warfare was based on bows and arrows, successfully resisted Dahomian attack in the 1750s (Dahomey blocked the supply of guns to them). Cavalry was more important to the north of the forest belt in West Africa, and it was largely thanks to cavalry that the kingdom of Oyo (in modern northeast Nigeria) was able to defeat Dahomey and force it to pay tribute from the 1740s. The Lunda of eastern Angola, who spread their power in mid-century, relied on hand-to-hand fighting, particularly with swords. The successful forces in the *jihad* launched by Usuman dan Fodio and the Fulani against the Hausa states in modern northern Nigeria in 1804 initially had no firearms and were essentially mobile infantry forces, principally archers, able to use their firepower to defeat the cavalry of the established powers. Their subsequent acquisition of cavalry, not firearms, was crucial in enabling them to develop tactics based on mobility, manoeuvrability and shock attack. By 1808, all the major Hausa states had fallen to the *jihadis*, indicating that firearms were not crucial in winning a war in Africa.[56]

In West Africa, furthermore, the Europeans remained confined to coastal enclaves, and not always in a satisfactory fashion. British cannon drove off Dahomey forces that attacked their fort at Glehue in 1728, but these forces had already captured the Portuguese (1727) fort there, and the French fort was partially destroyed by a gunpowder explosion in 1728. In 1729 and 1743, the Dahomians succeeded in capturing the Portuguese fort at Whydah, where Brazilian tobacco was exchanged for slaves. In 1761, the British Governor of Fort Louis, which had been captured from the French in 1758, reported 'the troops here are exceedingly sickly, and we have lost many officers and men, the whole garrison has suffered prodigiously ... it is not in my power to mount an officers' guard'.

The difficulties the Portuguese encountered in East Africa are also instructive. They regained Mombasa in 1728, after a mutiny by African soldiers against Omani control, but lost it again to the Omanis in 1729, with the Portuguese garrison capitulating as a result of low morale and problems with food supplies. Further south, the Dutch, expanding east from Cape Colony, overran the Hottentots and Bushmen with few difficulties, but then encountered the Xhosa, leading to a war between 1779 and 1781. The Xhosa put up serious resistance, but were defeated on the Fish River.

A major problem facing Europeans was a lack of knowledge about the African interior. This was only lessened from the close of the eighteenth century, with the Association for Promoting the Discovery of the Interior Parts of Africa, or African Association, being founded in London in 1788. The Association sought to explore the interior of Africa from the River Gambia. Daniel Houghton, an ex-army officer who had served at Gorée, went further beyond the River Senegal into the interior than previous European travellers, but his efforts to open a trade route were unsuccessful, and he was robbed; he died in 1791, well short of his goal, Timbuktu. From 1802, the government took over the sponsorship of the major expeditions from the Association. It supported Mungo Park, who, however, died in 1806 negotiating rapids on the River Niger. His *Travels in the Interior Districts of Africa* (1799) provided new information for mapmakers, as did William Browne's *Travels in Africa, Egypt, and Syria* (1800). In 1798, Francisco Lacerda e Almeida, the Portuguese Governor of Sena on the River Zambezi, concerned about the recent British conquest of Cape Colony against the Dutch, decided that the Portuguese needed to link their colonies of Mozambique and Angola. He reached Lake Mweru in central Africa, but died there of disease. This was the end of the attempt, although in 1806–11 two Portuguese mixed-race slave traders, Pedro Baptista and Antonio Nogueira da Rocha, did cross Africa from Cassange in Angola to Sena.

The problems faced by explorers were one aspect of the difficulties confronted by Europeans. Another was the vulnerability frequently felt on the peripheries of the European world, which led, for example, to the British Royal African Company seeking the support of warships. A sense of the precariousness of the European presence was conveyed by Captain William Cornwallis in a report to the British Admiralty about a voyage to the River Gambia in February 1775:

> I thought the appearance of a man of war might be of service. I therefore went up the river in the *Pallas* to James's Fort, which I found in great distress for want of stores, and particularly gun-carriages, not having above three or four serviceable ones in the Fort, and most of

their guns rendered totally useless for want of them ... I stayed in the River eight days, during which time we got the king of the country on board, and showed him all the civility we could; he seemed very well pleased, so I hope all will go on well again.[57]

Trade with Africa was only possible with the active cooperation of African rulers and others. Thus, the Scottish company that, from 1748 to 1779, ran a base on Bance Island near the mouth of the Sierra Leone River 'operated in a system that was largely structured by the Africans'. Co-operation extended, on the part of King Agaja of Dahomey, to an interest, in the 1720s, in permitting the establishment of European plantations in Dahomey. These were intended as a supplement to, rather than as a substitute for, the slave trade.[58] Co-operation was also the pattern for the Arab slavers based in ports such as Zanzibar, Kilwa and Mombasa, who played the key role in the Indian Ocean slave economy.

The relationship between foreign slavers and Africans was often a complex one. Within the wider context set by the European inability to coerce the Africans, there was an emphasis not simply on trade, but also on credit. This was more generally true of the European-dominated Atlantic trading system. Credit was given to encourage coastal Africans to purchase slaves from the interior. Mutual trust was important, but there was also a reliance on the security provided by the connections of the African traders who were left with the European merchants, and themselves shipped as slaves if they did not deliver.[59]

African rulers served the needs of a European-dominated Atlantic economy. The Atlantic economy pressed on the local, and the local served the global, and vice versa, with Anglo-African and Franco-African slave traders matching – and indeed, in West Africa, supplanting – their Luso-African equivalents.[60] In the valley of the River Senegal, patterns of trade between the desert and the savannah were annexed to the Atlantic world, as the export of slaves and gum arabic (a product used in textile manufacture that was the other major

European-controlled export from this region) reconfigured local economies and interregional trade. The cloth and metallurgical industries of West Africa were hit by European imports.[61] This foreshadowed problems that were to become more widespread in the nineteenth century.

There was a degree of African resistance to slavery, entailing both action against African slave hunters and against Westerners, the latter extending to 493 known risings on slave ships, especially in the late eighteenth century.[62] But this was far less significant than the active co-operation that fed the trade. Nevertheless, the prospect of risings on the ships ensured that crews were considerably larger (usually double) than on merchant ships of a similar size, and this affected the profitability of the trade. From this perspective, African resistance, or its threat, actively moulded the trade and limited the numbers transported. To that extent, the parallel with Jewish risings against the Holocaust is not that close.

The European position vis-à-vis slaves was far stronger in the Americas than it had been in Africa, although there were slave risings and problems created by escaping slaves. In 1739, in the Stono Rebellion in South Carolina, 100 slaves rebelled and killed 20 colonists, before being defeated by the militia and their Native American allies. The determination of some of the slaves to escape to Spanish Florida helped spark the rising. Although the scale varied, there were slave risings in the British West Indies: on Antigua in 1735–6, Jamaica in 1742, 1760, 1765 and 1776, Montserrat in 1768, and Tobago in 1770–4 (not an exhaustive list). Risings were usually brutally suppressed, and were followed by savage punishments and harsh retribution intended to deter fresh revolts. Alongside risings, there were also murders of individual overseers, as well as many suicides.

Circumstances, however, did not favour slave risings, as the whites restricted the availability of firearms and tried to prevent slaves plotting.[63] Frequent declarations of martial law served as a means of control in the British West Indies.[64] Indeed, slaves were unable to co-ordinate action, except in very small areas. In Pensacola in West Florida, which was under British rule from 1763 until it was regained by Spain in 1781, no slave was allowed out without his owner's written permission, and meetings of more than six slaves were forbidden after 9pm.[65] Those plotting what was to be known as 'Gabriel's Conspiracy' in Richmond, Virginia, in 1800 had first to consider how to acquire guns, horses and swords. In the event, the plan was betrayed by other blacks before the rising could take place.[66]

Flight was a more common form of resistance. It led, in Jamaica, to unsuccessful expeditions by British forces against the Maroons – runaway slaves who controlled much of the mountainous interior. The failure of these expeditions was followed, in 1738 and 1739, by treaties that granted the Maroons land and autonomy. Particularly in Brazil, but also elsewhere, there were organized communities of fugitive slaves, for example the 'Bush Negroes' of Surinam. A London newspaper, the *Briton*, in its issue of 11 December 1762, argued that gaining St Augustine in Florida from Spain would prevent 'the desertion of our Negro slaves' from Georgia. Further north, slaves fled to the Dismal Swamp on the Virginia–North Carolina border. Slaves who did not flee could, if circumstances were propitious, also engage in social protest and labour bargaining. A focus on this can sit alongside points made about the degree of peasant autonomy in Europe.[67] In Barbados during the eighteenth century, the insurrectionist attitudes that had led to plans for revolts in 1649, 1675 and 1692 were replaced by an emphasis on limited protest that was designed to secure the amelioration of circumstances. This contrasted with the other British islands, such as Jamaica, where circumstances were harsher.

The situation was generally less favourable than on Barbados. White concern about slaves reflected multiple anxieties. It was easy to misinterpret poor slave health or understandable black complaints about conditions as active defiance, and accordingly to react harshly. This contributed to the coercive nature of the slave economy and the reliance on force.

The circumstances of slave life, however, varied greatly.[68] At least some slaves, for example, became skilled men in the plantations, and hence acquired a self-respect that owners could recognize as a mutual advantage. Alongside the situation in Surinam, described by Candide, came the *Rule on the Treatment of Servants and Slaves*, introduced there by the Dutch in 1772 in order to counter slave unrest. This *Rule* was to be enforced by the Fiscal, an official to whom slaves had the right of appeal.

Regional variations in plantation economies had important consequences for the slave trade. In the case of British America, owing to the varied demands of tobacco and rice cultivation, and to related economic and social characteristics, slaves in the Chesapeake were more affected by white life, living as they did on relatively small farms, in close proximity to the owners; in the rice lands of South Carolina, on the other hand, there were fewer, but larger, plantations and the percentage of slaves was greater. In addition, the higher death rate ensured that, although by the 1750s the slave workforce could reproduce itself, the proportion of African slaves to American-born slaves was higher in South Carolina than in the Chesapeake. As a consequence, in South Carolina, slaves were more autonomous and more influenced by African culture and material life, and relations between slaves and whites remained more antipathetical than where they lived in closer proximity, although it is not easy to assess slave attitudes.[69]

The slave situation in Jamaica, where slaves were also treated harshly, was more akin to South Carolina than the Chesapeake: among both slaves and whites in Jamaica, the majority were immigrants. The diaries of Thomas Thistlewood, who was a slave owner and agricultural manager in west Jamaica from 1750 to 1786, indicate clearly that he treated his slaves cruelly, not least by abusing his female slaves sexually. Similarly, on Sir William Stapleton's profitable sugar estate on Nevis there were very exploitative working arrangements, and in the 1730s the black population fell by nearly 25 per cent. In the British Windward Islands – Dominica, Grenada, St Vincent and Tobago – in the 1760s and early 1770s, treatment was harsh and did not encourage family life and reproduction, in large part because it was easier to buy new slaves than to raise children to working age. The resulting regime led to high mortality and low fertility, with far too little food provided to slaves. The severity of treatment contributed to flight and suicides.[70]

The slave situation in Brazil was also more similar to that in South Carolina and the West Indies than Chesapeake. The growing need for slaves in South Carolina and Georgia helped ensure that the balance of the British slave world shifted, so that, by 1775, there were more slaves in British North America than in the British West Indies. In part, this also reflected the amelioration of the slave position in the Chesapeake, which led to a higher rate of natural increase, and which was to become more apparent in the nineteenth century.

Differing needs for slaves were a key aspect of variety, and fed through into slave flows. Rising prices for slaves in British North America from mid-century indicate that demand was outstripping supply. For example, the Ibo shipped from the Bight of Biafra were favoured by Virginia planters, but were seen as insufficiently strong by Carolina and Georgia planters, who preferred Bambara and Malinke from Senegambia, or Angolans. In South Carolina, Georgia and East Florida, opinion among planters about slavery was divided. The better established commercial agriculture was, the more its participants wanted to reform or diversify it, especially to prevent greater dependence on slavery. Conversely, newer settlers welcomed such dependence.[71] Indeed, the relationship between slavery and economic development could be very varied. Thus, in the lower Mississippi in the 1760s, Spain and Britain, the new rulers in Louisiana and West Florida, respectively, took measures to increase the number of colonial inhabitants, both white settlers and black slaves, and an export economy developed, based on indigo, tobacco and timber.[72]

The treatment of slaves was related to the racism of the period. Racist attitudes were by no means restricted to the unlearned. Of some importance were religious and biological explanations for apparent racial differences, whose genesis could be traced back to the sons of Adam, with blacks being the children of the cursed Ham. Influential writers argued in favour of polygenism – the different creation of types of humans. This led to suggestions that blacks were not only a different species, but were also related to great apes, such as orang-utans. This was related to the argument that, although blacks were inherently inferior, they were particularly well adapted to living in the tropics. Physical attributes, particularly skin colour, attracted much attention. Montesquieu and Buffon explained colour as a function of exposure to the tropical sun. The ability of blacks to cope better than whites with diseases in the tropics was believed to exemplify an inherent difference that was linked to a closeness to the animals that lived there. This was held to justify slavery, and the same argument was used about the alleged nature of African society. For example, in his *A New Account of Some Parts of Guinea and the Slave Trade* (1734), William Snelgrave defended the trade on the grounds that being offered up as a sacrifice was the alternative for those taken prisoner in African conflicts – an argument that was to be adopted by opponents of abolition later in the century.

The argument that bile was responsible for the colour of human skin, advanced as a scientific fact by ancient writers, was repeated without experimental support by eminent eighteenth-century scientists, including Buffon, Feijoo, Holbach and La Mettrie. An Italian scientist, Bernardo Albinus, proved to his own satisfaction in 1737 that Negro bile was black, and in 1741 a French doctor, Pierre Barrère, in his *Dissertation sur la cause physique de la couleur des Nègres*, published experiments demonstrating both this and that the bile alone caused the black pigment in Negro skin – a topic that was discussed in *The Gentleman's Magazine* the following year. This inaccurate theory won widespread acclaim, in part thanks to an extensive review in the *Journal des Savants* in 1742, and played a major role in the prevalent mid-century belief that blacks were another species of man without the ordinary organs, tissues, heart and soul. In 1765, the chief doctor in the leading hospital in Rouen, Claude Nicolas Le Cat, demonstrated that Barrère's theory was wrong, but he was generally ignored and Barrère's arguments continued to be cited favourably.[73] They accorded with a hierarchical classification of humanity that served the interests of the slave trade.

It is instructive that the most successful sentimental critique of slavery published in early eighteenth-century Britain related not to a black slave, but to a Native American. The tale of 'Inkle and Yarico', published on 13 March 1711 in the leading periodical, the *Spectator*, was one of humanity affronted, and morality breached, by slavery:

> Mr. Thomas Inkle, an ambitious young English trader cast ashore in the Americas, is saved from violent death at the hands of savages by the endearments of Yarico, a beautiful Indian maiden. Their romantic intimacy in the forest moves Inkle to pledge that, were his life to be preserved, he would return with her to England, supposedly as his wife. The lovers' tender liaison progresses over several months until she succeeded in signalling a passing English ship. They were rescued by the crew, and with vows to each other intact, they embark for Barbados. Yet when they reach the island Inkle's former mercantile instincts are callously revived, for he sells her into slavery, at once raising the price he demands when he learns that Yarico is carrying his child.

This was but a stage in a tale that had surfaced in Richard Ligon's *History of the Island of Barbados* (1657), and whose iterations were to include George Colman the Younger's much-performed play *Inkle and Yarico* (1787), which, in the fashion of the time, was provided with a happy ending.[74]

The popularity of the story reflected the way in which the transoceanic world could provide a setting for moral challenges. Slavery was an important instance, but, prior to the late eighteenth century, there was an ambivalence in the treatment of blacks. The portrayal of blacks could be sentimentalist, and the harsh world of their work and lifestyle was generally ignored, although this criticism could also be advanced in the case of the extensive artistic treatment of the

European peasantry. Joseph Wright's intimate and gentle portrayal of *Two Girls with their Black Servant*, which may have been his *A Conversation of Girls* exhibited in 1770, probably depicts the daughters of a merchant in Liverpool, where Wright worked in 1769–71. The service depicted here seems agreeable, and bears little reference to the grimmer nature of reality.

Slavery was banned by the Trustees of the new colony of Georgia in 1735, not so much out of hostility to slavery as out of a desire to base the colony on small-scale agrarian activity, rather than on aristocratic plantations. Defensive considerations also played a role, and the law was entitled 'An Act for rendering the Colony of Georgia more defensible by prohibiting the importation and use of Black Slaves or Negroes into the same'. The colonists, however, opposed the measure from the outset, not least because they had to watch their South Carolina neighbours getting rich using cheap labour, while they could barely eke a living. The Malcontents, the leading political faction in Georgia that opposed the Trustees, published several pamphlets calling for legalization of the slave trade, but they were unsuccessful. The Stono Rebellion in South Carolina was cited by the Trustees. They, however, finally capitulated in 1750, arguing that, since Spain had been unsuccessful in 1742 when it invaded Georgia from Florida during the War of Jenkins' Ear (1739–48), it was safe to import slaves. This compromise followed concessions on other restrictions, such as on land tenure and alcohol consumption. It was an aspect of the collapse of the Trustees' position, and they surrendered their charter in 1752.[75] Their objective of creating a colony of virtuous small farmers had not been realized, but it prefigured the goal of Thomas Jefferson. Trustees wanted silk or wine as their monoculture, but neither worked out very well. The economy of Georgia only came close to being a success after the Trustee era, and real wealth had to wait for King Cotton.

By the end of the century, most advanced opinion no longer regarded blacks as a different species of man, but as a distinct variety. This interpretation, monogenesis – the descent of all races from a single original group – was advanced by Johann Friedrich Blumenbach, a teacher of medicine at the University of Göttingen, who, in 1776, published *De Generis Humani Varietate*, an influential work of racial classification that went through several editions. However, the misleading assessment of the inherent characteristics of non-Europeans, combined with the association of reason with European culture, encouraged a hierarchy dominated by the Europeans, and thus a treatment of others as inferior. Thus, although monogenesis can be seen as a benign theory that could contribute to the concept of the inherent brotherhood of man that was voiced during the Enlightenment, and especially in the period of the American and French Revolutions, it was also inherently discriminatory. Blumenbach assumed the original ancestral group to be white, and theorized that climate, diet, disease and mode of life were responsible for the developments that led to the creation of different races.

Characteristics and developments were understood in terms of the suppositions of European culture, and this led to, and supported, the hierarchization already referred to. This also tended to be true of the developing idea of cultural relativism, although subversive themes could be offered, as by the British painter William Hogarth, in his *Analysis of Beauty*. He pointed out that 'the Negro who finds great beauty in the black females of his own country, may find as much deformity in the European beauty as we see in theirs'.[76]

Among 'advanced' thinkers, notions of brotherhood were subordinated to a sense that Enlightenment and revolutionary ideas and movements originated within the Western world. Irrespective of the nobility of outsiders, their societies appeared deficient and defective, and thus inferior. This was seen in writing on history and sociology, for example William Robertson's influential *History of America* (1777).

At the same time, black subjects of European powers who were not slaves were increasingly granted civil rights. The French made efforts to incorporate free blacks as subjects, following Louis XIV's *Code Noir* of 1685. In 1761, Asian and East African Christian subjects of the Portuguese Crown were given the same legal and social status as Portuguese whites, on the grounds that subjects should not be distinguished by colour. Pombal, the leading Portuguese minister, explicitly cited the classical Roman model of colonization: citizenship had eventually been granted irrespective of origins. However, extending rights for non-whites in Goa, a long-established Portuguese colony, where syncretism and mutual interest were both important, provided no guidance to the more coercive treatment of slaves and Native Americans in Brazil.

The combination of these views with economic interest helped ensure that the cause of freedom in the case of American liberty did not extend to the slaves.[77] Dedicated to the most prominent French radical, Jean-Jacques Rousseau, the third edition of Thomas Day's *The Dying Negro* criticized the American Patriots for supporting slavery, a theme he returned to in his *Reflections on the Present State of England and the Independence of America* (1782). The Hessian soldiers sent to fight the Americans felt that the Americans' treatment of their slaves formed a hypocritical contrast with their claims of the equality of man.

There was, moreover, increased criticism of slavery among progressive intellectuals. The *Encyclopédie* (1751–65) had been characterized by contradictory or tentative views, alongside criticism, for example by Jaucourt in his entry on slavery.[78] In contrast, Abbé Raynal's influential *Histoire philosophique et politique des établissements et du commerce des Européens dans les deux Indes* (1770) became, especially in its 1774 and 1780 editions to which Denis Diderot made important contributions, a channel for the expression of progressive ideas, such as anti-slavery.[79] The *Histoire* was condemned by the Inquisition in Spain, but was widely read by European reformers, for example in Italy. It was also translated into English.

The use of black soldiers in conflict against whites proved a particularly sensitive issue. In a 1741 letter intercepted by the British, Etienne de Silhouette, a French agent in Britain, reacted with alarm to the news that the British were arming blacks in order to use them against Spanish-ruled Cuba. He felt this might be very dangerous for all American-Europeans, but argued that the British were too obsessed by their goals to consider the wider implications.[80] In practice, the issue did not become important until the War of American Independence (1775–83), when the British were very short of manpower, which led them to turn to Native Americans, Loyalists and German-subsidy troops, in order to make up for the shortage of regular troops. In November 1774, James Madison, a prominent Virginian, warned:

> If America and Britain should come to a hostile rupture I am afraid an insurrection among the slaves may and will be promoted. In one of our counties lately a few of those unhappy wretches met together and chose a leader who was to conduct them when the English troops should arrive – which they foolishly thought would be very soon and by revolting to them they should be rewarded with their freedom. Their intentions were soon discovered and proper precautions taken to prevent the infection. It is prudent such attempts should be concealed as well as suppressed.

He returned to the theme the following June:

> It is imagined our Governor [John, 4th Earl of Dunmore] has been tampering with the slaves and that he has it in contemplation to make great use of them in case of a civil war in this province. To say the truth, that is the only part in which this colony is vulnerable; and if we should be subdued, we shall fall like Achilles by the hand of one that knows that secret.

That summer, Jeremiah Thomas, a black ship's pilot who himself owned slaves, was sentenced to death in South Carolina for supplying arms to the slaves and encouraging them to flee to the Dutch.[81] Later that year, Dunmore added Loyalists and blacks to his forces, seizing the towns of Gosport and Norfolk. He issued a proclamation emancipating slaves who joined his army, creating an 'Ethiopian Regiment' of several hundred escaped slaves, but he was defeated at Great Bridge on 9 December 1775. General Prevost armed 200 blacks at the time of the American-French siege of Savannah in 1779, a step that was criticized by the Americans.[82] When the British threatened Charleston in May 1779, a large number of slaves fled to their camp in search of promised freedom, and, during the city's siege in 1780, the British encouraged slaves belonging to Revolutionaries to run away. The slaves of Loyalists were returned to their masters on condition they were not penalized, but the slaves of Revolutionaries were to work on sequestered estates or perform other designated tasks, in return for which they would receive their freedom at the end of the war. Fleeing slaves were punished by the Revolutionaries. The first three to be captured, attempting to flee to Dunmore in 1776, were publicly hanged, decapitated and quartered.

Towards the end of the war, there was increased interest in the idea of black troops. In January 1782, Dunmore backed John Cruden's proposal to arm 10,000 blacks, who would receive their freedom under white officers. Two months later, the British commanders at Charleston proposed raising a black regiment.

Although inexperienced in the use of firearms, blacks acted with success as irregulars, fighting on the eastern shore of the Chesapeake alongside Loyalist partisans. Others, calling themselves the King of England's soldiers, fought on from the swamps by the River Savannah after the British had evacuated Charleston and Savannah. In May 1786, a combined force of militia and Catawba Native Americans defeated them, but, a year later, a Governor's message mentioned serious depredations of armed blacks 'too numerous to be quelled by patrols' in southern South Carolina.[83]

The British failure to employ blacks for military purposes on any scale can be regarded as an opportunity missed. However, it would have greatly complicated the British position in the South, where there was a need to mobilize Loyalist support. It was also necessary to consider the impact on the West Indies. In November 1779, William, 2nd Earl of

Shelburne, a key member of the opposition, warned the House of Lords about the danger of arming Jamaican blacks.[84]

As yet, there was not the large-scale use of black troops that was to be seen in the French Revolutionary and Napoleonic Wars.[85] Neither situation was of direct significance for the state of the slave trade or slavery, but both American independence and the use of black troops underlined the dynamic nature of circumstances and the extent to which the trade was affected by external factors.

Although the American constitution did not end slavery, it did make provisions for the end of the slave trade. Furthermore, slavery was slowly abolished in the states of the North. However, with the exception of Massachusetts, this did not involve the emancipation of slaves, but rather, as in New York under legislation of 1799, the freeing of slave children born thereafter once they reached maturity.[86] The bulk of the black population (which was 19.3 per cent of the national population in 1790), nevertheless, was in the South.

Alongside the continuation of slavery, there was also much harsh treatment of other workers that led to comparisons with slavery. Travelling from Füssen in Bavaria to Innsbruck in Austria in 1787, Adam Walker wrote of the women he saw: 'I sincerely pity them, they are such slaves as I have heard the Negroes in the West Indies described. No uncommon sight to see them threshing corn, driving wagons, hoeing turnips, mending the highways.'[87]

It would not have benefited the slaves to know that they were part of a more dynamic economic system, in which consumerism, capital accumulation, and investment in industrialization were all linked.[88] For example, profits accumulated in Glasgow from sugar and tobacco trading helped fund the development of the chemical industry in west-central Scotland, and also increased the liquidity of Scottish banks. This was an aspect of the extent to which the British Atlantic stood out from the other European Atlantics in terms of the combined degree and intensity of the processes of exchange and linkage.[89]

CHAPTER 4

THE NINETEENTH CENTURY

The nineteenth century witnessed the end of legal slave trading in the Atlantic world, and that is the major topic of attention; but it should be noted at the outset that this process was not without considerable opposition and faced serious difficulties. Nevertheless, the abolitionist cause did succeed, first against the slave trade, and then against slavery. The debate over abolitionism, and therefore the arguments for and against, can be traced back to the eighteenth century. Among the key abolitionist currents were religious pressure and secular idealism. The first was particularly important in the Protestant world, although there had always also been a significant current of Catholic uneasiness about, and sometimes hostility to, slavery.

In Protestant Europe, the slave trade was abolished first by Denmark in 1792. This was achieved by government decree (without an abolitionist campaign), although the law did not come into force until 1803, and, in the meanwhile, the slave population in the Danish West Indies (now the American Virgin Islands) was built up from about 25,000 to about 35,000. In part, it was believed in Denmark that Britain and France would soon abolish the trade and would then seek to prevent other powers from participating, which proved to be an erroneous expectation in the short term. The Slave Trade Commission in Denmark also argued that slave conditions on the islands would improve if imports were banned, as it would be necessary to look after the slaves in order to encourage them to reproduce. In short, slavery would become less reprehensible – a view also taken by British abolitionists.[1]

In addition, in the Protestant world, criticism of the slave trade and slavery developed in the Netherlands.[2]

Changes in Britain were more important, because of her position as the leading European imperial and naval power, due to her key role in the slave trade and in the Caribbean slave economy, and thanks to her potential influence on other states. Christian assumptions about the inherent unity of mankind, and about the need to gather Africans to Christ, played a major role in influencing British opinion. Missionary activity among slaves became significant from the mid-eighteenth century, and the Methodist leader, John Wesley, strongly attacked both slavery and the slave trade in his *Thoughts upon Slavery* (1774). In 1791, he was to send William Wilberforce a dying message, urging him to uphold the abolitionist cause. In polite society, by the early 1770s, both slavery and the slave trade were increasingly seen as morally unacceptable.[3]

Commercial benefits from the abolition of the slave trade were also predicted by some commentators, Malachy Postlethwayt arguing, in his *The Universal Dictionary of Trade and Commerce*, that the trade stirred up conflict among African rulers and thus obstructed both British trade and 'the civilising of these people'.[4] Belief in such benefits became far stronger in the early nineteenth century, as British merchants looked for new export markets, particularly in the face, first, of the Napoleonic attempt to weaken Britain by banning her trade with Europe and, subsequently, of Continental protectionism, for example the German *Zollverein* (Customs Union) established in 1834. Furthermore, the massive expansion of British industry meant that there were more goods for sale, as well as a desire for raw materials. Thus, a very different basis for trade with Africa was proposed.

Lord Mansfield's ruling, in the case of James Somersett in 1771–2, that West Indian slave owners could not forcibly take their slaves from England, made slavery unenforceable there, and was matched by a reluctance among Londoners to help return runaway slaves. The legal status of slavery in Britain, however, was still unclear. Abolitionist sentiment, directed against the slave trade, became more overt from the 1780s, and was an aspect of the reform pressure and religious revivalism of the period. Quakers played a prominent role, but they and others were effective, in part, because of a more widespread shift in opinion. In 1787, a national lobbying group, the Society for the Abolition of the Slave Trade, was established. The pressure it exerted contributed to the Dolben Act of 1788, under which conditions on British slave ships were regulated. The ready responsiveness of the slave trade to the change in circumstances was speedily demonstrated: the restrictions imposed under the Dolben Act led to an increase in the costs to the slave trader and encouraged the use of larger ships, on which there were economies of scale to be made. In 1789, a similar (but less rigorous) act was passed by the Dutch, and in 1799 British restrictions were strengthened.

Abolitionist sentiment affected the arts, and led to the production of visual and literary images of the horrors of slavery, such as the medallion of the Society for the Abolition of the Slave Trade designed by William Hackwood and manufactured at Josiah Wedgwood's factory. There was a mass of pamphlet literature and discussion of the issue in humanitarian novels, as well as comments on the abolitionist fight. Information on the slave trade and the colonies was sought by abolitionists, leading to Thomas Clarkson's *The Substance of Evidence on Sundry Persons in the Slave Trade* (1788).

The prolific abolitionist literature struck both Evangelical and rational notes. Key works included Clarkson's *An Essay on the Slavery and Commerce of the Human Species, Particularly the African* (1786), the translation of a Latin prize dissertation at Cambridge, and Thomas Burgess's *Considerations on the Abolition of Slavery and the Slave Trade, Upon Grounds of Natural, Religious, and Political Duty* (1789). Much is made of the Methodist and Evangelical campaigns and arguments for abolition, but Burgess, the leading Anglican advocate of abolition, wrote one of the most powerful and comprehensive attacks on slavery. At the time of writing, he was a Fellow of Corpus Christi College, Oxford, and a prebendary of Salisbury, where he was later

Bishop. Burgess advanced religious arguments, but also encompassed wider philosophical and political contentions. His book declared the 'Good effects, which would follow from the abolition of slavery, in preparing the way for the diffusion of Christianity and Civilization in Africa, a liberal and extended communication between Africa and Europe, and the discovery of the interior parts of Africa.' In opposition, the Society of West India Merchants and Planters sponsored pamphlets in favour of the trade.

The controversy reached into the distant corners of the country. On 7 April 1789, for example, the *Leeds Intelligencer* reported the collection of £18 in support of the application to Parliament for repeal of the trade 'raised by voluntary contributions in a small part of the high end of Wensleydale ... The contributors (being chiefly farmers) were informed of the injustice and inhumanity of the slave trade by pamphlets circulated previous to the collection.' Across the country, the press resounded with the battle: for example *Swinney's Birmingham and Stafford Chronicle* of May 1791 included a poem by 'H. F.' praising William Pitt the Younger's recent parliamentary speech on the slave trade.

Pressure to abolish the trade, however, was hindered by the importance of the West Indies to the British economy, as well as by the opposition of George III and the House of Lords. Dolben's Bill, for example, was bitterly opposed in the Lords by the Lord Chancellor, Lord Thurlow, a favourite of the King, while other ministers, such as Lord Hawkesbury, the President of the Board of Trade and another favourite, and Viscount Sydney, the Home Secretary, offered more muted opposition. In 1791, Wilberforce's motion to bring in a bill for the abolition of the trade was defeated in the House of Commons by 163 to 88. The following year, his motion for abolition in 1796 was passed by 151 to 132, but the Lords postponed the matter by resolving to hear evidence. In 1793, Wilberforce's motion to hasten the actions of the Lords was rejected, as was that to abolish the supply of slaves to foreign powers. In 1794, the latter motion passed the Commons, but was rejected in the Lords. In 1795, the Commons refused leave to bring in a bill for abolition, and in 1796 a bill was rejected on its third reading. In 1797, 1798 and 1799, efforts also failed. In 1804, the measure passed the Commons, but was defeated in the Lords, while, in 1805, it failed its second reading in the Commons.

There was also a populist tone to opposition to abolition, one that is too often overlooked. In William Dent's cartoon 'Abolition of the Slave Trade, or the Man the Master', published in London on 26 May 1789, produce is shown waiting for a purchaser because its price has gone up, while a slave in Western clothes beats a semi-clothed white, saying 'Now, Massa, me lick a you, and make you worky while me be Gentleman – curse a heart.' Whites are depicted at work in the sugar fields, while blacks feast under the words 'Retaliation for having been held in captivity'. As a reminder of international competition, a foreigner remarks 'By gar den ve sal have all de market to ourselves, and by underselling we sal send Johnny Bull's capitall and revenue to le Diable', while a Briton comments: 'Why, if I have my rum and sugar and my tobacco at the old price – I don't care if the slave trade is abolished.'[5]

Part of the opposition to abolitionism derived from the continued conviction that slavery was compatible with Christianity, and also that it was sanctioned by its existence in the Old Testament. For example, the Dutch Reformed Church, the established Church in Cape Colony, argued that slaves were not entitled to enter the Church, and that conversion to Christianity would not make slaves akin to Europeans, because they had been born to slavery as part of a divine plan. The Dutch settlers opposed missionary activity among their slaves; the same was true of plantation owners in the West Indies.[6] By 1800, there were nearly 17,000 slaves in Cape Colony, brought by sea from the Indian Ocean.

To supporters of slavery, an acceptance of blacks as fully human did not preclude slavery. Instead, they were presented as degraded by their social and environmental backgrounds. In part, opposition to abolition more specifically reflected the conservative response in Britain to reform agitation after the

French Revolution, which broke out in 1789. The Revolution had been linked to a secular idealism that had embraced abolitionism as one of its themes. In February 1788, *La Société des Amis des Noirs* had been founded, with help from British abolitionists. Although the French were far less active than their British counterparts, the *Société* pressed for the abolition of the slave trade and, eventually and without compensation, of slavery. One of its founders, Jacques-Pierre Brissot, argued that, with education, blacks had the same capacities as whites.[7]

In the utopian idealism of the French Revolution, the liberties affirmed by the Revolutionaries were believed to be inherent in humanity, and thus of global applicability. In January 1792, the attention of the National Assembly was directed by its Colonial Committee towards Madagascar. Instead of a French territorial expansion to be achieved by conquest, there was a call

> not to invade a country or subjugate several savage nations, but to form a solid alliance, to establish friendly and mutually beneficial links with a new people ... today it is neither with the cross nor with the sword that we establish ourselves with new people. It is by respect for their rights and views that we will gain their heart; it is not by reducing them to slavery ... this will be a new form of conquest.[8]

Initially, however, the slave trade was not banned by France; indeed, it reached its peak during the years 1789–91. This reflected the value of the West Indies to the French economy. It was argued that slaves were not French and, therefore, that slavery and revolution were compatible. The major rising in France's leading Caribbean colony, Saint-Domingue, in 1791 altered the situation, and also helped competing sugar-producing areas: the British colonies and, especially, Brazil. This rising led to a complex conflict in Saint-Domingue in which, in 1793, the Civil Commissioner, Léger Sonthonax, freed the slaves in the Northern Province in order to win their support. The following year, the National Convention abolished slavery in all French colonies, a step that was unwelcome to most of the white settlers.[9]

This idealism, however, did not protect the French position in Saint-Domingue, which, instead, after a bitter war, became the independent black state of Haiti. There were important African echoes in the rising and the subsequent warfare, but the revolt also drew on European practices and on the ideology of revolutionary France. Toussaint, the leader of the rising, captured the Spanish side of the island in 1800. His forces were defeated by the French, in part because Toussaint was treacherously seized during negotiations; however, his successor, Jean-Jacques Dessalines, drove the French out in 1803.[10] Fighting in Haiti demonstrated what was also seen with the British West Indies regiments: that blacks were far better than Europeans as warriors in the Caribbean, particularly because their resistance to malarial diseases was higher.[11] Prefiguring their very different later role in subsequently ending the slave trade, the British played an important part in ensuring the success of the Haitian revolution, with a crucial blockade of Saint-Domingue's ports in 1803, when war between the two powers resumed. This wrecked the French attempt to recapture the colony.

There were also slave revolts elsewhere in the Caribbean world in the 1790s, including, in the British colonies, Fedon's rebellion on Grenada in 1795–6, and risings or conspiracies in Dominica and St Vincent, followed by a conspiracy on Tobago in 1802.[12] All were unsuccessful, as was the Pointe Coupee slave rebellion in Louisiana in 1795. However, the success of the Haiti revolution led to a climate of fear in white society, which was intensified by the killing of settlers on Grenada in 1795. The Maroons of Dominica, who were already a serious problem in 1785, were only suppressed in 1814, in part as a result of defections and, in part, due to the burning of their cultivated patches.

French revolutionary idealism also fell victim to the reaction and consolidation associated with Napoleon: slavery was restored in Guadeloupe and Martinique in 1802, and the entry to France of West Indian blacks and mixed race people was prohibited.[13] Slave rebellions were less successful in Latin America than in Saint-Domingue. The 1798 small-scale 'Revolt of the Tailors' in Salvador in Brazil, which included slaves as well as mulattos and whites, called for the abolition of slavery, but it was brutally suppressed against a background of widespread white fears.[14]

The situation in Britain differed from that in France. There was a boom in sugar exports caused by the chaos in Saint-Domingue, and the popularity of abolitionism was affected by the widespread opposition to populist reform that stemmed from hostility to the French Revolution. Thereafter, however, there was, in contrast to France, an upsurge in abolitionism in the 1800s, and this led to the formal end of the British slave trade.[15]

The end of the slave trade and of slavery itself has, by some commentators, been ascribed to a lack of profitability, caused by economic development, rather than to humanitarianism.[16] This view, however, underplays the multiplicity of factors that contributed to it. Some studies attribute much significance to economic problems in the plantation economy of the West Indies – problems stemming from the impact of the American Revolution (and subsequent protectionism) on the trade between North America and the West Indies that was so important to the latter's supplies and markets.[17] There are, however, also contrary indications that slave plantations in the West Indies remained profitable.[18] In part, this reflected the ability of plantation owners to innovate. An aspect of this innovation included better care for the slaves, which helped ensure that the British colonies were approaching demographic self-sufficiency by the 1820s, and were thus less in need of the slave trade. This matched the situation in the USA, and underlines the extent to which the end of the trade did not necessarily weaken slavery.

At the same time, in the West Indies, the cost of acquiring and sustaining the workforce rose, due partly to moves against the slave trade, and partly to market forces; and by the time of emancipation, the material consumption levels of the slaves were similar to those of manual workers in Britain.[19] Aside from its continued profitability, the West Indies' plantation economy anyway remained an important asset base. Furthermore, the limited convertibility of assets did not encourage disinvestments from slavery: too much money was tied up in mortgages and annuities that were difficult to liquidate in a hurry, and the planters had a good case for the generous compensation they pressed for (and received), rather than the loan originally proposed.

Instead of problems within the slave economy, it is more appropriate to look at the outside pressures for abolition, which led, indeed, to a situation in which it became the general assumption of the 'official mind' that action against the trade was a proper aspect of British policy.[20] These pressures included, and contributed to, a marginalization of groups, especially West Indian planters, that had encouraged and profited from British, and indeed European, demand for tropical goods. The reforming, liberal, middle-class culture that was growing in importance in Britain regarded the slave trade and slavery as abhorrent, anachronistic, and associated with everything it deplored. Abolitionists, indeed, were encouraged and assisted by a confidence in public support, and this helped influence the debate amidst the élite. Abolitionism offered the country, tired as it was by the travails of seemingly intractable war with Napoleon, the opportunity to feel itself to be playing a key role in the advance of true liberty, and the abolitionist medals show just how self-conscious this was.[21] This was particularly valuable in 1806, as Britain's allies succumbed after French victories at Austerlitz (1805) and Jena (1806). All sorts of reform impulses in Britain converged on abolitionism, including concern over the treatment of animals.[22]

In 1805 the ministry of William Pitt the Younger, a statesman who profited from his appeal to this reforming middle-class constituency, issued Orders-in-Council that banned the import of slaves into newly captured territories after 1807 and, in the meantime, limited the introduction of slaves to 30 per cent of the number already there. This proclamation was taken much further by the next government, the more reformist 'Ministry of All the Talents', which took power after Pitt's death in early 1806. That year, the new ministry supported the Foreign Slave Trade Act, ending the supply of slaves to conquered territories and foreign colonies. This was presented on prudential grounds, as a way of limiting the economic strength of these territories when some were returned as part of the peace settlement at the end of the war, as they certainly would be: Cuba, Guadeloupe and Martinique had been returned by Britain in 1763, and the last two were to be returned after the Napoleonic Wars.

The highpoint of the abolitionist process occurred when the Abolition Act of 1807 banned slave trading by British subjects and the import of slaves into the other colonies. The relevant divisions were 283 to 16 in the Commons, and 100 to 36 in the Lords, and the bill received the royal assent on 25 March 1807. Subsequently, in 1811, participation in the slave trade was made a felony.

Britain also used its international strength to put pressure on other states to abolish or limit the slave trade, for not only did the trade now seem morally wrong, but, once abolished for British colonies, it was also seen as giving an advantage to rival plantation economies. Naval power, amphibious capability, and transoceanic power projection ensured that the British were in a dominant position and well placed to advance their views. Once war broke out again with Napoleon in 1803 – a war that lasted until 1814, and was briefly and successfully resumed in 1815 – the British seized St Lucia, Tobago, Demerara and Essequibo (now both in Guyana), and Surinam in 1803–4, following up with the Danish West Indies – St Croix, St Thomas and St Johns in 1807, Martinique and Cayenne in 1809, and Guadeloupe, St Eustatius and St Martin in 1810. Fort Louis, the last French base in Africa, fell in 1809.

Although the pressure they exerted, both during the Napoleonic Wars and afterwards, was widely resented by others as self-interested interference and undesirable moralizing, the British were in a position to make demands. In 1810, Portugal, then very much a dependent ally, protected from

Napoleon by British troops, came under pressure to restrict the slave trade as a preliminary to abolition; because Brazil and Angola were Portuguese colonies, the Portuguese position was important. In 1815, on his return from Elba, Napoleon abolished the French slave trade, possibly as a way to appeal to progressive British opinion. Subsequently, after he was defeated at Waterloo, the returned Bourbon regime of Louis XVIII in France, like Portugal a dependent ally, was persuaded by Britain to ban the slave trade again. This was of great concern to British abolitionists, as the French slave trade, if it had continued, would have offered an opportunity for British investment. Under British pressure, the Congress of Vienna issued a declaration against the trade.[23] In 1817, an Anglo-Portuguese treaty limited the slave trade in Brazil to south of the Equator, ending the supply of slaves from the Guinea coast, and an Anglo-Spanish treaty contained similar provisions (Spain having rejected such pressure in 1814). In 1814, with effect from 1818, the Dutch slave trade was abolished. Again, this reflected British influence, as the Netherlands was also a dependent ally.

In 1807, with effect from 1 January 1808, the slave trade was also prohibited by the United States, but there was scant effort to enforce the ban. Orders-in-Council, however, issued on 11 November 1807, were used by the British to justify seizing American slavers. The High Court in 1810 accepted the argument of the barrister James Stephens, Wilberforce's brother-in-law and a member of the Clapham Sect, who had become convinced of the horrors of slavery during his time in the West Indies. Stephens argued that slave trading was a violation of the law of nations, the laws of humanity and Anglo-American law, and that, therefore, neutral slave ships that had been captured could be legitimately seized.[24] During the war of 1812, the British willingness to receive and arm escaped slaves aroused American anger. British commentators suggested encouraging slave resistance as a way of weakening the USA. In 1814, Viscount Sidmouth, the Home Secretary, received a proposal that the British change the politics of America by turning to the slaves: they were to be emancipated in Virginia and Maryland, which was to be supported as a separate country.[25]

The Atlantic slave trade continued, however, not least because *slavery* had not been abolished. British participation in the trade persisted, both legally and illegally, directly and indirectly. This included the purchase of slaves for British colonies and British-owned operations elsewhere (such as mining for gold in Brazil and for copper in Cuba), the provision of goods, credit, insurance and ships to foreign slave traders, and direct roles in slavery. Delays in emancipation enabled British and other investors to continue to invest in other slave systems, and helped maintain the profitability of the slave trade. They also encouraged purchases designed to pre-empt the end of legal imports. The provision of capital was particularly valuable to slave societies, which otherwise found it difficult to obtain sufficient capital, and this was an aspect of Britain's dominance of what was otherwise an undercapitalized Atlantic world. As also in free societies, British finance helped support rail construction, and this was important to plantation economies in Brazil, Cuba and the USA. The British were not alone in this process. American manufactured goods supplied to Africa came to play a significant role in the slave trade from the 1840s.[26]

Although demand for labour was, in large part, met from the children of existing slaves, the continuation of slavery ensured that, even where the slave trade had been abolished, smuggling continued, although it was not very extensive in the British West Indies. An illicit slave trade continued in the French Atlantic world, especially Cayenne (French Guiana), and also in the French Caribbean. The French undertook at least 193 slaving voyages between 1814 and 1820, although there were few after 1831. Deception extended to the shipping of slaves termed *libertos* by the Portuguese and *engagés à temps* by the French. The French financed their trade with the export of goods to Africa, but this was a small flow compared to that from Britain.[27]

In response to action against the trade, however, there was a need to search for new sources of slaves, and this led to the development of South-East Africa – a distant source, where the slaves were, in part, purchased in return for textiles shipped from Bombay. However, distance hit profitability, and, as a result, most slaves shipped via the Portuguese bases in Mozambique, such as the ports of Mozambique and Quelimane, went to nearby Mauritius and Réunion, and not to Brazil.

Demand kept the trade alive. More particularly, the slave trade to the leading and increasingly important market of Brazil was not effectively ended until 1850, and that to the second market, Cuba, until 1867. Cuba, which, until conquered by the USA in 1898, was a Spanish possession, imported an annual average of 10,700 slaves in 1836–60. The profitable nature of the sugar economies of Brazil and Cuba, the commitment to the lifestyle and ethos of slave holding, and a lack of relevant European immigrant labour all kept the trade successful. Demand encouraged supply, as well as shifts in the supply system. For example, the number of slaves shipped through Portuguese-controlled ports in the Cabinda region rose in the 1820s. In part, this was due to the decline of the French and Dutch trade from this region, but it was also partly a result of the expansion of the Atlantic slave trade further east, into the African interior.[28] American slavers profited greatly from demand in Brazil and Cuba.

Until the late 1830s, the Bight of Benin and, until the 1850s, the Angolan coast north to Cabinda remained important sources of slaves. The export of slaves to Brazil helped ensure that, whereas in 1801–20 about 1,153,000 slaves crossed the Atlantic, in 1821–43 the figure was 1,486,000, a higher annual average.[29] The role of the British in the Bight had been taken by Brazilian, Dutch, Portuguese and Spanish traders. Furthermore, the raiding warfare that provided large numbers of slaves remained important across Africa, and responded to shifts in the Atlantic transit system.[30] For example, Opubu the Great, ruler of the important port of Bonny on the Bight of Biafra (1792–1830), responded to British moves against the slave trade by selling palm oil to Britain, while, at the same time, developing his slave interests with Portugal.[31]

The flow of slaves to Brazil was principally financed by the shipping of textiles, cheap brandy and firearms to Angola. Britain and Brazil were the leading sources of the textiles; Britain's role was important to Anglo-Brazilian trade, and helped complicate the attitudes of the British government to the continuation of the slave trade, with pressure on the issue coming from British manufacturing interests. The textile trade also helped spur Brazilian production. As a result of the continued flow of new slaves, Brazil and Cuba remained more African in the nineteenth century than the British West Indies or the southern USA. In terms of their societies and cultures, this had important long-term consequences that continue to this day.

In the USA, the initial acceptance of slavery was a product of the federal character of the new state, and of the role of slave holding, not only in the economies of the Southern states, but also in their sense of identity and distinctiveness. When the Union was originally created, it had been agreed that abolition of the slave trade would take place, an abolition agreed in 1807, but there was no such provision for slavery. The importance of the loyal border states (Delaware, Maryland, Kentucky and Missouri) was such that, even on 1 January 1863, when President Abraham Lincoln declared that Union victory in the Civil War would lead to the end of slavery, this related only to the Confederacy, and not to those states.

The slave trade to the USA was no longer legal, but, within that country, the extent of the slave states ensured that there was still a very extensive slave trade, particularly from the Old to the New South – a situation similar to that in Brazil, where the sugar planters of the North-East sold slaves to the coffee planters further south, who were expanding west into the province of São Paulo, using the railway to create new links and opportunities.[32] Similarly, delays in emancipation provided a market for the slave trade within the Caribbean, particularly once direct trade with Africa was limited. Caribbean slave supplies, for example, became more important to the Spanish colony of Puerto Rico from 1847.[33] Aside from slave sales, the prevalence of slave hiring in the

American South ensured considerable geographical mobility among slaves. This helped keep slavery responsive to the market, and thus an economic system. Without a trade in slaves, there would have been no room for such entrepreneurship, nor for the interaction with capital that purchase and hiring offered.[34]

The slave economy in the USA was transformed as a result of the major expansion of cotton. This owed much to Eli Whitney's invention in 1793 of the cotton gin, a hand-operated machine that made it possible to separate the cotton seeds from the fibre. This encouraged the cultivation of 'upland' cotton. This variety was hardy, and therefore widely cultivable across the South, but was very difficult to de-seed by hand, unlike the Sea Island cotton hitherto grown, but which had been largely restricted to the Atlantic coastlands. As a result, annual cotton output in the USA rose from 3,000 bales in 1793 to over three million in the 1850s.[35]

The profitability of the cotton economy was important to the continued appeal of slavery in the South, and, as tobacco became less well capitalized, so slaves from the tobacco country were sold for work on cotton plantations. This ensured that slaves became less important in the Chesapeake states. Nevertheless, the success of the cotton economy and the ability to boost the birth rate of American slaves were such that Southern apologists did not regard the slave system as anachronistic. While Texas was under Mexican rule (1821–35), the attempt by the Mexican government to prevent the import of slaves there aroused much anger among the American colonists.

Britain expended much diplomatic capital on moves against the slave trade, so that the granting of recognition to the states that arose after the collapse of Spain's empire in Latin America depended on their abolishing the slave trade. British support was important to abolitionism in formerly Spanish America, but so also was the example and process of rebellion against Spain that had led to independence. These rebellions challenged existing patterns of authority, but also saw a breakdown of order far greater than that in the

American War of Independence, and one that was exploited by many slaves in order to escape or rebel. Indeed, slavery itself was abolished in Chile in 1821 and in Mexico in 1829. In Argentina, Peru and Venezuela, abolition was a gradual process.

British recognition of the then-independent Republic of Texas in 1840 was made on the same basis of abolition of the trade. Pressure was also exerted on other states, including France and the USA, to implement their bans on the trade, although there was considerable anger on their part about British demands, not least over the issue of searching ships. Indeed, British pressure was partly countered by the continuation of slavery in the USA, and American influence, in particular, helped in the ongoing slave trade to Cuba. So also did the lack of a Spanish abolitionist movement.

In 1839, the Palmerston Act authorized British warships to seize slave ships registered in Portugal and sailing under the Portuguese flag, a measure in part intended to hit the use of the flag by Brazilian slave dealers. Some traders then switched to the French flag. New treaties to enforce the end of the trade were signed with Portugal in 1842 and with France in 1845.[36]

This issue caused particular problems in Anglo-Brazilian relations. In 1826, Brazil, concerned about its international position, accepted a treaty with Britain, ratified in 1827, that promised to make the trade illegal within three years of ratification. Furthermore, in 1831, the Brazilian General Assembly passed a law ordering the liberation of all slaves entering Brazil. In anticipation of abolition, the treaty led, in 1828–30, to a marked rise in demand for slaves, and also in their price. There was also renewed interest in the recruitment of Native Indian labour. Demand for slaves and prices fell in 1830–3, though both rose again later.

This reflected the pathetic nature of enforcement, which proceeded from a strong sense that slavery and the slave trade were essential – a sense that drew on the continuing demand for slaves, as well as anger over British interference and Brazilian measures to enforce the law. In the late 1830s, political pressure for the end of restrictions on the trade grew, and was openly conducted. The Brazilian navy came to do very little against the trade. The low price of slaves in Africa encouraged the revival of the trade. The inflow of slaves into Brazil greatly increased, to an annual flow of over 50,000 in the late 1840s (the annual average in 1826–50 was 38,000), so that by 1850 there were over two million slaves in Brazil.[37] Many worked in the booming coffee industry, which benefited from increased demand from the growing population of Europe.

In 1845, however, the British Parliament passed a Slave Trade Act, which authorized the British navy to treat suspected slave ships as though they were pirates. This led to the pursuit of ships into Brazilian waters, much to the anger of Brazil. However, the Brazilians were in no position to resist Britain, either politically or economically: coffee and sugar could have been obtained by Britain elsewhere, and Brazil needed British capital. Greater British pressure was exerted from 1850, when the slave trade was formally abolished by Brazil under the Eusébio de Queiroz law, a measure that owed much to British action. The British subsidized Brazilian abolitionism. More generally, by pushing up the price of slaves, which rose greatly in the 1850s and yet more thereafter, British pressure helped ensure that slave owning became too expensive for many Brazilians, and this reduced the role it could play.[38]

Pressure was also brought to bear on the Spanish colony of Cuba – enough for David Turnbull, the Consul, to be accused of inciting slave risings.[39] This underlined the extent to which slavery came to an end in slave societies as a result of external pressures, and was an instance of a more general characteristic of slavery – the extent to which it was moulded by such pressures.

The sense of moral purpose behind British policy rested on the state's unchallenged naval power,[40] and this policy was given a powerful naval dimension by the anti-slavery patrols off Africa and Brazil and in the West Indies. Indeed, in 1807, when Britain was at war with France and naval resources were very stretched blockading its ports, two warships were sent to African waters to begin the campaign against the slave trade.

Furthermore, abolitionists pressed for the retention of bases in West Africa that could help in action against the trade.

In part, the use of naval pressure against the Barbary states of North Africa, which seized Europeans as slaves, acted as a bridge that helped to make such pressure against Western traders elsewhere seem more acceptable. In 1816, in the biggest deployment of this type, Admiral Lord Exmouth and a fleet of 21 British warships, with the support of a Dutch frigate squadron, demanded the end of Christian slavery in Algiers. When no answer was returned, the fleet opened fire. Some 40,000 roundshot and shells destroyed the Algerine ships and much of the city, the Dey yielded, and over 1,600 slaves, mostly from Spain and the Italian principalities, were freed. This was seen as a great triumph. Exmouth was made a viscount, voted the freedom of the City of London, and was granted membership of chivalric orders in Naples, Sardinia, Spain and the Netherlands.[41]

The British presented themselves as acting on behalf of the civilized world, and as assuming a responsibility formerly undertaken by the Bourbon powers. In 1819, a British squadron returned anew to Algiers, and, in 1824, the threat of bombardment led the Dey to capitulate again to British demands. That year also, the Bey of Tunis was made to stop the sale of Christian slaves. This was very different to the scale of British action in the eighteenth century, although, in 1739, Rear-Admiral Haddock had been ordered to Algiers to support the Consul in demanding the release of enslaved British subjects.

The most important active British anti-slavery naval force in the first half of the century was that based in West Africa (until 1840 part of the Cape Command), which freed slaves and took them to Freetown in Sierra Leone, a British colony for free blacks. The anti-slavery commitment led to a major expansion of this force from the 1820s to the 1840s. In the late 1830s, British naval action helped greatly to reduce the flow of slaves from the Bight of Biafra.[42] Warships based in Cape Town, a British possession from 1806, also played an important role, and anti-slavery patrols were extended south of the Equator in 1839, enabling Britain to enforce the outlawing of the slave trade Brazil had promised in 1826 but had failed to implement. In 1839, unilateral action was taken against Portuguese slavers after negotiations failed. The achievements of the warships were celebrated in Britain, and the capture of the slave schooner *Bolodora* by HMS *Pickle* in 1829 inspired a painting by William Huggins that was engraved by Edward Duncan.

Anti-slaving activities were not restricted to the Atlantic, but were also important in the Indian Ocean and in East Asian waters. Thus, in 1821–3, the frigate HMS *Menai*, based at Mauritius, took action against slavers. There were also operations against piracy, which was often focused on slave-raiding, for example off Sarawak in northern Borneo. In 1843–9, HMS *Dido* and other warships joined James Brooke in stamping out pirates who were resisting his influence there.

Public abolitionist sentiment remained strong in Britain and encouraged government action. This sentiment was directed against both foreign activity and British participation, for example in the Brazilian mining industry.

The advent of steam power added a new dimension to the naval struggle. It increased the manoeuvrability of ships, making it easier to sound inshore and hazardous waters, and to attack ships in anchorages. This made a major difference in the struggle against the slave trade, as slavers were fast, manoeuvrable and difficult to capture, and could take shelter in inshore waters. It was also necessary for the British navy, from the 1840s, to respond to the use of steamships by slavers keen to outpace the patrols. In 1851, Lagos, a major West African slaving port fed by the serious Yoruba civil wars, was attacked and the slaving facilities destroyed, with the steamship *Penelope* playing a prominent role. Lagos was annexed by Britain a decade later. In the 1830s, Macgregor Laird, who founded the African Steamship Company, sought to use steamships to make the River Niger in West Africa a commercial thoroughfare for British trade, which he hoped would undermine the slave trade. This was also a theme of Sir Thomas Buxton's *The African Slave Trade and its Remedy*

(1839), and of the Society for the Extinction of the Slave Trade and for the Civilisation of Africa.

The role of the British navy ensured that opposition to the slave trade would not simply be a matter of diplomatic pressure. It also meant that there was a constant flow of news to help keep abolitionism at the forefront of attention in Britain. The role of the navy also demonstrated the extent to which external pressures were crucial to the end of the slave trade.

Alongside the teleological tone of much writing about action against the slave trade, one should note the problems and criticisms. On 12 July 2006, the *Times* reported on the recently discovered journal of the young Lieutenant Gilbert Elliott, the son of the Dean of Bristol, who had been a naval officer on HMS *Sampson*, and had served on the slave patrol. Critical of the laws, Elliott claimed that abolition had been poorly conceived: 'I should very much like to freight a ship with Philanthropists and send them to sea – to show them … what dreadful misery it has brought on those poor unfortunate savages whose condition they pretend to better.' Elliott argued that the blockade was ineffective and that, therefore, it would be better to permit the trade to resume: 'I am one of those who believe that while there is a demand there will be a supply, and that nothing will stop the trade unless we ruin the slave powers.' Elliott was horrified by the conditions of liberated Africans, who were kept in barracoons – coastal forts – while awaiting movement: 'thousands of poor wretches huddled together where no sea breeze can blow on them'. At the same time, this was scarcely the fault of the navy, and Elliott's account of Africans who were freed underlined the plight caused, or exacerbated, by enslavement, including malnutrition, ill-health and exhaustion.

The American navy also took part in the struggle against slavery, sometimes in co-operation with the British. This action overlapped with the protection of trade against privateering and piracy. The combined goals led to a major American naval commitment to the Caribbean from the 1820s, with operations offshore and onshore at Cuba, Puerto Rico, Santo Domingo and the Yucatán. In 1822, Commodore James

Biddle commanded a squadron of fourteen American ships in the Caribbean, and in 1823 David Farragut won notice in command of a shore party in Cuba while on anti-slavery duties. American naval activity also ranged further afield. In 1843, sailors and marines from four American warships landed on the Ivory Coast in West Africa in order to discourage the slave trade and to act against those who had attacked American shipping. The Dutch navy, in contrast, made little effort against slave traders. Once Brazil had prohibited the trade in 1830, Brazilian warships played a role, although it met with scant government support and was soon restricted.

Aside from action against the trade itself, pressure was brought to bear on African rulers to agree to end the slave trade and, instead, consent to legitimate trade.[43] This was an aspect of a more general interest in deriving benefit from inland Africa. For example, in 1812, Major-General Charles Stevenson sent Robert, 2nd Earl of Liverpool, Secretary for War and the Colonies, a memorandum urging the need to gain control of Timbuktu on the River Niger:

> Africa presents a new country and new channels for your industry and commerce, its soils favourable for your West India productions, it produces gums, drugs, cotton, indigo ... gold ... iron ... this to England is infinitely of more consequence than the emancipation of South America ... the teak wood so famous for ship building might be cultivated with success in some of its various soils ... the possession of Timbuktu would secure you the commerce of this quarter of the world and give you a strong check upon the Moorish powers of the Mediterranean by being able to intercept all their caravans and refusing them the commerce of the interior. It would likewise give you a complete knowledge of Africa to the borders of the Red Sea and to Ethiopia ... at the same time you could raise black armies for your East Indies ... not destined to conquer Africa, but bridle it, in order to have a check upon its kings, to protect British commerce as well as the African in its transit

through the different kingdoms, by which means we should hold the country in check without the expense of defending it and by good management make the greater part of its sovereigns our friends, by supporting some, protecting others and augmenting their powers, and, as allies, drawing from them whatever black battalions we may want.[44]

As with the ongoing slave trade, in Africa Western pressure had to be exerted with due regard to the continued strength of its rulers. This was brought home in 1821, when the 5,000-strong British Royal African Colonial Corps under Colonel Sir Charles McCarthy, Governor of Sierra Leone, was destroyed by a larger, more enthusiastic and well-equipped Asante army. The Governor's head, which became a war trophy and was used as a ceremonial drinking cup, provided a particularly lurid illustration of Western failure. McCarthy's replacement, Major-General Charles Turner, recommended total withdrawal from the Gold Coast, but, instead, the British withdrew to hold only Cape Coast Castle and Accra.[45] The Company of Merchants Trading to Africa was abolished that year and their bases were transferred to the government.

New methods did not necessarily bring success in increasing Western control in Africa. In 1816, an expedition sought to travel up the River Congo, in order to discover if it was the outlet of the River Niger. Led by Commodore James Tuckey in command of the *Congo*, the first steamship on an African river, the expedition was blocked by difficult cataracts on the river, the boat did not operate correctly, and Tuckey and many of his men died of disease. No further progress was to be made until 1877, when Stanley completed the first descent of the River Congo.

Indeed, in the 1810s and 1820s, Egyptian expansionism in North-East Africa was more obviously successful than European efforts in West Africa. This Egyptian expansionism continued to be important into the 1870s, with Darfur, Equatoria and Harrar all acquired in that decade. Slave raiding and trading were aspects of this spreading Islamic control.[46] It was only from the 1840s that European power really became more insistent on the West African coast. French imperialism developed, with colonies established in Gabon (1842) and Ivory Coast (1843), while Spain established another, Rio Muni, the basis of the modern state of Equatorial Guinea, in 1843.

Paradoxically, the slave trade was ended just as the ability of Western states to project power into the African interior became stronger. This prefigured the later, very different, case of Western colonialism receding after World War Two, at a time when absolute Western military power had reached an unprecedented level. Slavery also came to an end when attitudes of racial superiority and Social Darwinism were becoming more clearly articulated.

The French expanded their strength in the valley of the River Senegal from 1854, developing an effective chain of riverine forts linked by steamboats.[47] Having had their 1864 expedition against the Asante wrecked by disease, the British launched a successful punitive expedition against them in 1873–4. Benefiting from superior weapons – Gatling guns, seven-pounder artillery and breech-loading rifles (against Asante muskets) – they defeated the Asante at Amoafu (1874) and burned down their capital, Kumasi. The assistance of other African peoples, especially the Fante, was also important in this campaign.[48] At the same time, enslavement continued in Africa as an aspect of warfare there. For example, in what is now Botswana, the expanding Ngwato kingdom conquered and enslaved the Sarwa.[49]

It is very easy to move from the abolition of the Western slave trade to that of slavery, but it is important to note that these were not simultaneous, and that there were cross-currents. In pressing, in 1792 and 1807, for abolition of the slave trade, Wilberforce had denied that he supported immediate emancipation, as he considered the slaves not yet ready. Abolitionists had hoped that the end of the slave trade would lead to greater care of the remaining slaves by their owners, and to the withering of slavery.

In contrast, there is a sense that the slave world was being strengthened at the very time that the slave trade was being ended. This was true not only of Mauritius in the Indian Ocean but also of the colonies of Demerara-Essequibo and Berbice on the Guiana coast of South America, seized by the British from the Dutch in 1803. Plantation agriculture, the large-scale importation of African slaves, and a switch from cotton and coffee to sugar, all followed British conquest there,[50] as also occurred on Trinidad, seized from Spain by Britain in 1797. Thus, these colonies were more like those of the late seventeenth-century West Indies than the more mature slave societies of the West Indies of the time, where a lower percentage of the slaves were African-born and where the work regime was less cruel.[51]

The continued strength of slavery contributed to fresh abolitionist pressure in Britain from the mid-1820s. In 1823, the Commons passed a resolution for the gradual abolition of slavery, although it was modified in the parliamentary process to take more note of the planters' interests. The Anti-Slavery Society was also founded that year. This pressure was mirrored in the West Indies by slaves keen to gain their freedom: some believed that their owners were withholding concessions granted by the Crown. Slave owners, in turn, showed no desire to end slavery. Indeed, in 1830-1, there was talk in Jamaica of secession from British rule in response to abolitionist pressure in Britain and legislation aimed at the owners' powers of discipline over their slaves.

Racism remained strong in the Caribbean world, and was brutally displayed in the harsh suppression of slave rebellions, as on Barbados in 1816 (Bussa's rebellion), in Demerara in 1823, and on Jamaica in 1831-2, the Baptist War, this last being partially a response to pro-slavery agitation among the white population. This was the largest slave rising in the British West Indies.[52] In the French colony of Martinique, there was a major rising in 1831.

There were also slave risings in Virginia in 1800 and 1831, Louisiana in 1811, and South Carolina in 1822, the Denmark Vesey conspiracy, which included a plan for the seizure or destruction of Charleston. The American determination to end slave flight from Georgia to Florida lay behind the Seminole Wars (1817–18, 1835–42, 1855–8), as the Seminole Native Americans in Florida provided refuge for escaped slaves.[53] Indeed, in the second war, an armistice came to an end in 1837, and Seminole resistance revived, when the Americans allowed slavers to enter Florida and seize Seminole and blacks. In contrast, an important success for the Americans was scored in 1838, when Major-General Thomas Jesup announced that blacks who abandoned the Seminole and joined the Americans would become free; this cost the Seminole 400 black fighters.

Religious zeal played an important role in slave risings in this period, for example on Jamaica and around Bahia in Brazil between 1808 and 1835: the 1835 Bahia revolt was of Muslim slaves and freedmen.[54] Opposition was also expressed in murders, flight and suicide, and each was frequent. The conditions of slave labour in Brazil, especially in the North-East, remained harsh and often violent, particularly in the sugar and coffee plantations. Food and clothing for the slaves was inadequate, and the work was remorseless, hard and long. Death rates among slaves were high, partly on account of epidemic diseases, but also partly due to the work regime, which was not abated in harsh weather. The conditions of work for pregnant women led to many stillbirths, and mothers lacked sufficient milk. However, the 1872 census showed that 30 per cent of slaves worked in towns, and conditions were better there. More humane treatment of rural slaves only began in about 1870, when their price rose.[55]

In Cuba (like Brazil, a low-cost producer), slavery remained important to the sugar monoculture of much of the economy, especially in the west of the island. The sugar economy depended on American investment, markets and technology, while the British embrace of free trade helped Cuban production by ending the preferential measures that helped ensure markets for sugar from Britain's colonies. Some British plantation owners emigrated to Cuba.

In Britain, abolitionist tactics reprised those earlier directed against the slave trade, with press agitation, public meetings and pressure on Parliament. Concern about the plight of Christian slaves made the issue more potent, as did decreased confidence that the end of the slave trade would lead to the end of slavery. Pressure grew for immediate emancipation, instead of gradual improvement. Reports of the slave rising in Jamaica in 1831–2, and of the brutality with which it was suppressed, helped make slavery appear undesirable and redundant. The Whig ministry that pushed through the Great Reform Act of 1832, which revised the electoral franchise in favour of the middle class, also passed the Emancipation Act of 1833, with slaves emancipated from 1 August 1834, Emancipation Day. The slave owners were financially compensated. Many Whig candidates had included an anti-slavery platform in their electoral addresses, and Whig victories in the general elections of the early 1830s were crucial. The bill received its royal assent on 28 August 1833.

The Reform Act contributed directly to this legislation, as many seats traditionally occupied by members of the West Indies interest were abolished and, in their place, came constituencies that favoured abolition. These seats tended to be large or medium-sized industrial or shipping towns, especially those with Nonconformists.[56] The debate on abolition itself did not follow party lines. Most of the (opposition) Tories did not play a role in the debate, and nor did they vote against the government. Instead, the West Indies interest played a crucial role, and much of the debate revolved around the financial issue of compensation. The latter was raised to a grant of £20 million, which strengthened the planters' position in the West Indies. Furthermore, initially, as a transition, all slaves aged over six were to become apprenticed labourers, obliged to work for their former masters for forty-five hours a week: field workers for six years and others for four. A clause, however, forbade the punishment of former slaves. This interim system, which led to protests from many former slaves, was ended in August 1838.

But this was far from the end of the story as far as Britain was concerned. The already strong opposition to the slave trade elsewhere was joined by action directed against slavery in other countries. Anti-slavery agitation continued after the Emancipation Act, with the Anti-Slavery Society being particularly influential.

Anti-slavery was less important and popular in most of Continental Europe, whether in Catholic France or in the Protestant Netherlands, partly because of the lack of a public politics comparable to Britain's.[57] In France, the *Société de la Morale Chrétienne*, founded in 1821, was small, and a disproportionately high percentage of its members were Protestants. However, in the more liberal July Monarchy that followed the 1830 revolution, laws were passed in 1833 ending the branding and mutilation of slaves and giving free blacks political and civil rights. Effective action against the French slave trade was also taken, largely because the new government was readier to ignore popular complaints about British pressure.

The end of slavery in the French colonies followed in 1848. The British example was important in weakening French slavery, not least because it provided French slaves with new opportunities for escape to British colonies where there was no slavery. The increased influence of reforming middle-class circles was important in France, but the decisive pressure came from a small group of writers and politicians, especially Victor Schoelcher, who argued for immediate emancipation, rather than the slow process that had long been favoured. As an instance of the latter, in 1845, the Mackau laws had been restricted to helping slaves towards self-purchase.

There have been efforts to ascribe French abolition to slave unrest in the country's colonies. This is contentious. It diverts attention from the crucial metropolitan context of decision-making, but major uprisings in Martinique and Guadeloupe in 1848 certainly speeded the application of emancipation, and the argument that revolt was a possibility was pushed hard by French abolitionists.[58] As in Britain and Denmark, there was compensation for the slave owners.

In 1848, slavery in the Danish West Indian islands (now the American Virgin Islands) was abolished when the threat of rebellion among the slave population forced the Danish Governor-General to free the slaves. Sweden had done the same the previous year for its colony of St Barthélemy, while much of formerly Spanish America abolished slavery in the 1840s and 1850s. There followed the Dutch colony of Surinam in 1863, the USA in 1865 (with the Thirteenth Amendment to the Constitution), Spain in its colony of Cuba in 1886 (emancipation gradually began in 1870), and, most importantly, Brazil in 1888.

Already the majority of blacks in Brazil were free: manumission had been increased under the Law of the Free Womb or Rio Branco law of 1871, which stated that all future children born to slave mothers would become free from the age of 21 (a clause that led to false registrations by owners), and, in addition, slaves were allowed to purchase their freedom. Slavery was regarded in influential circles, especially in the expanding cities, as a cause of unrest (which indeed increased in the 1880s), and a source of national embarrassment and relative backwardness. As part of the process by which New World settler societies were culturally dependent on the Old World, the élite looked to Europe to validate their sense of progress, and were affected by the extent to which slavery was increasingly presented as an uncivilized characteristic of barbaric societies, and as incompatible with civil liberty. Furthermore, slavery was seen by some, particularly the growing industrial lobbies, as an inefficient system compared to wage labour. The combination of the end of the slave trade and economic expansion meant that slavery was no longer able to supply Brazil's labour needs, including those in the traditional centre of slavery, the North-East, and this helped make it seem anachronistic. Not only was quantity of labour an issue, but also type, as a growing need for artisans was not one that could be met from the traditional Brazilian slave economy.

This was an aspect of the degree to which modernization led to the demise of slavery – not only culturally and ideologically, but also for economic reasons. However, at the same time, Western economic growth had helped provide the demand, the finance and the technological innovation that kept slavery a major option, and this is a reminder of the ambivalent relationship between modernization and slavery. Nevertheless, as the role of slavery declined in the Brazilian economy, and with it the role of slaves in the net capital of that economy, so it seemed anachronistic and a legacy issue. As a result, slave owners became increasingly isolated, with free labour becoming more important even in some plantation areas, such as São Paulo, although there was also a continued preference for slave labour in others. The end of the slave trade had led to higher slave prices and a concentration of ownership,[59] and this reduced political support – a process similar to that in the American South. This lessened the stake of the wider economy in the slave trade.

In 1884, two Brazilian provinces emancipated slaves, creating free labour zones, and in 1885 all slaves over the age of 60 were freed. Furthermore, increased numbers of slaves fled, many to cities such as Rio de Janeiro, so that, by 1887, there were fewer than one million slaves: only about five per cent of the Brazilian population. There was far more support for slave flight than in the USA, with much of the populace, as well as the bulk of the authorities, unwilling to support the owners. This contrasted markedly with the situation in the USA – a contrast that was very important to the subsequent history of the two countries. Because, in Brazil, the slave owners were without a mass domestic constituency, their eventual position was more similar to that of their counterparts in the Caribbean than to those in the American South. In Brazil, the military was not keen on hunting escaped slaves, and there was nothing like the serious Southern separatism based on slavery found in the USA. This was a key aspect of the largely non-violent nature of Brazilian abolitionism. There was no equivalent to the situation in Cuba, where the Ten Years' War of 1868–78, an unsuccessful independence struggle against Spanish rule, had seen partial abolition in rebel areas, which encouraged the move towards gradual abolition on the island as a whole.

Whereas in the American South there was an emphasis on white society (an emphasis that was to encourage racial exclusion, whether slave-based or not, as a form and focus of Southern cultural identity), in Brazil, by contrast, the stress was on a multicultural society. In Brazil, the 1888 Golden Law, passed by an overwhelming majority in Parliament, freed the remaining slaves, about three-quarters of a million in total, with no compensation for owners. This law helped legalize the situation caused by large-scale flight, and has also been seen as an attempt to retain workers on the land.[60]

The end of slavery in the Western world, however, did not completely transform labour relations, either in Britain's colonies or in other former slave societies such as Brazil.[61] Control over labour continued. In the British colonies, as elsewhere, many former slaves were pressed into continuing to work in sugar production.[62] Legal systems were employed to restrict the mobility and freedom of former slaves, for example by limiting emigration or by defining what was regarded as vagrancy. Rents were also used to control labour and to reduce labour costs. Resistance took the form of striking and leaving the plantations. The new system was supported by punishment, including the use of workhouses, where the harsh regime acted as a potent form of control. For example, once female apprentices entered the workhouse, they were no longer protected by the Abolition Act.[63] The difficult situation for workers in the British colonies after 1838 undercuts any simple attempt to create a contrast between slavery and freedom,[64] although, on the other hand, very different notions of liberty were involved as a result of the abolition of slavery. The conditions of labour for slaves and ex-slaves reflected far more than just the legal situation:[65] across the world, for most former slaves, there was no sweeping change in their lives, and many remained dependent, in some form or another, on their ex-masters or on new masters.

Despite the abolition of the slave trade and slavery, labour continued to flow to the colonies. Former slaves tended to take up small-scale independent farming, on provision grounds, rather than work on plantations, and this helped bring about demands for fresh labour. Meanwhile, the very flexibility of economic service and subjugation ensured the continuation of systems of labour control, and these encompassed labour flows. The same was true of Russia, where, in 1861, Tsar Alexander II emancipated the serfs. In place of slaves, the British West Indies, especially Trinidad, British Guiana (now Guyana) and other colonies, received cheap Indian indentured labour. For example, nearly a quarter of a million indentured Indians moved to British Guiana from 1838 to 1918, and 150,000 to Trinidad between 1845 and 1917. Critics claimed that the indentured labour systems, which were also employed in Cuba and the French Caribbean, represented a continuation of the slave trade in its latter stages, not least due to the coercive character of these systems. Despite work-force availability, however, sugar production declined.[66]

Dependence on new or former masters was also the case for many former slaves in the USA. A new order had certainly been seen with Union victory in 1865. In the second half of the Civil War, the recruitment of all-black regiments for the Union army, numbering more than 120,000 men, had been both a major operational help to the Union, and a symbol of what, to the Confederacy, was indeed a total war. Black troops had been given combat roles, the action at Fort Wagner in July 1863 proving a key watershed; and sometimes made up the bulk of a force. The symbolic power of black troops had been shown in 1865, when the forces that occupied Charleston, the site of the outbreak of the war, included black troops recruited from former Carolina slaves. Larger numbers of slaves had escaped as the advance of Union forces brought disruption to the South, not least with General Sherman's advance across Georgia in 1864. And in 1865, the Thirteenth Amendment to the Constitution had led to the freeing of about four million slaves.

However, the Reconstruction Acts of 1867, which dissolved the Southern state governments and reintroduced federal control, were not sustained. Federal troops were withdrawn from the South in 1877, the black militias recruited by

Radical Republican state governments lost control or were disbanded, and the blacks in the South were left very much as second-class citizens – a situation that persisted until the 1950s and 1960s.[67]

Despite the introduction of Indian indentured labour, the former plantation societies of the West Indies and British Guiana became far less important to the British economy. This was a process accentuated by the equalization of the sugar duties in 1846, under the Sugar Duties Act – a free trade measure, in accordance with which protection for British sugar was progressively reduced until all duties on imported sugar were equalized in 1851.[68] The Act encouraged sugar imports into Britain from Brazil and Cuba.

The abolition of slavery played a major role in the crisis of the British plantation societies, and this was particularly marked in Jamaica. Labour availability and discipline were crucial to the ability of estates to hold down costs. With emancipation, productivity and profitability fell, as, despite the possibilities offered by the adoption of steam power in the shape of steam milling, sugar production continued to be labour-intensive. Free labour proved more expensive and less reliable than slaves, which greatly increased operating costs. In Jamaica, 314 estates, 49 per cent of the sugar plantations, ceased cultivation between 1844 and 1854, and there was insufficient investment in the others. Similarly, in Brazil, the end of slavery hit the sugar economy of the North-East as a key aspect of a more general agrarian depression that affected the old order in Brazil, weakening the monarchy. Brazil became a republic in 1889.

As the exports of the former British plantation economies declined, so they were less able to attract investment, afford imports from Britain and elsewhere, and develop social capital; and this had an impact on the living standards of the bulk of the population of these colonies. In 1815, the West Indies had been the leading market for British exports, but by 1840 it had been passed by India, Australia and Canada, in that order,[69] and the role of the West Indies in British shipping needs also diminished. The decline of the plantation economies indeed contributed to the fall in the empire's share in British trade, although the expansion of trade with other countries outside the empire also played an important part in this relative decline. In the former slave colonies, the problems centred on slavery had changed, not ended, as was to be made clear in Jamaica by the harsh (and illegal) suppression of the Morant Bay uprising in 1865.

The end of the trans-Atlantic slave trade also led to the development of plantation economies in parts of Atlantic Africa, particularly Angola. This represented a response to labour availability in Africa, but also reflected a shift in the terms of Western trade with Africa, away from a willingness to pay for labour in the shape of slaves, and toward one to pay for labour in the form of products. There continued, indeed, to be multiple overlaps between servitude and trade in the Atlantic African economy.

In West Africa, the end of the slave trade hit those kingdoms that had derived wealth from it; meanwhile, the slave trade increased in East Africa, seriously affecting much of the interior of the continent.[70] This reflected the slave-based plantation systems that developed on Africa's Indian Ocean coast, producing, for example, cloves, the export of which boomed in the 1810s–40s. Furthermore, the export of slaves to the Islamic world continued, for instance to Arabia. Kilwa was the leading port in East Africa, with a major trade from there to the Persian Gulf, much of it handled by Omani merchants. Their profits helped finance economic activity, which, in turn, produced needs for slave labour. Slaves to Arabia, in contrast, were moved relatively short distances, particularly from the Red Sea ports of Suakin and Massawa, which were fed by slave raiding and trading into Sudan and Ethiopia. As in the New World, slave labour in East Africa was largely plantation labour, but the situation was different in Arabia and the Persian Gulf. This serves as a reminder of the economics of slavery, and of the variety of slave conditions, and therefore the slave experience. Slaves there were used for many activities, but there was no dominance by large-scale institutions of the plantation type, although slaves were used for date plantations in Oman. Instead, slaves represented a mobile labour force that could be used for different needs.

As slaving was largely brought to an end in the Atlantic in the 1860s, so the British struggle against it in East African waters became more prominent, with the Cape Squadron being allocated to the task and, in 1864, merging with the East Indies Squadron. This struggle with Arab slavers was presented in a heroic light and was fully covered in British publications, including newspapers. It was also deemed worthy of having books published about it, such as Captain George Sulivan's *Dhow Chasing in Zanzibar Waters* (1873) and Captain Philip Colomb's *Slave-Catching in the Indian Ocean* (1873). The slaves of Indian traders in East Africa were confiscated by the British Consul in 1860, as the traders were British subjects.

Opposition to slavery was not restricted to the oceans, but also encouraged moral activism towards Africa, especially hostility to the slave trade in Central and East Africa. This hostility had a number of consequences, including the development of a British presence in Zanzibar,[71] and a strengthening of the determination to blaze the trail for Christian grace and morality, seen, for example, in the actions of, and response to, David Livingstone, who helped secure British pressure to persuade the Sultan of Zanzibar to outlaw the slave trade in 1873. HMS *London*, an old ship of the line, was sent to Zanzibar to enforce this ban, and the acquisition from Germany of Zanzibar itself as a protectorate in 1890, in exchange for the island of Heligoland in the North Sea, led to the end of the trade.

Colonies for free Africans, many freed slaves, also developed. Sierra Leone, established by the British in 1787, was the first. Both the Committee for the Relief of the Black Poor and key government supporters appear to have been motivated in founding this colony by humanitarianism, springing from Christian convictions, gratitude towards Loyalist blacks from the former North American colonies, and abolitionist sympathies; and the settlement explicitly forbade slavery. The great majority of newspaper items covering the venture were sympathetic in tone. Combined with intermarriage and the good public response to the appeal for money to help poor blacks, this suggests that racial hostility may have been less common than has often been assumed.[72] Subsequently, slaves freed by the British navy were taken to Sierra Leone.

The British were not alone. In 1849, the French founded Libreville in Gabon for freed slaves. The American equivalent, Liberia, in contrast, was an independent republic, originally established by an anti-slavery group, the American Colonization Society (founded in 1816), as a home for freed American slaves. The first settlers landed in 1821, although, once they became established, they were harsh in their treatment of the local Africans. Colonists were taken to Liberia by American warships. In part, Western backing for these states rested on a support for the removal of blacks from white countries, a support that could align abolitionist sympathies with a hostility to multiculturalism.

In Africa, the treatment of slaves held within native society became more problematic as the Europeans became colonial rulers across most of the Continent. They were committed to abolition as part of the civilizing mission used to justify imperialism as progressive, but this risked offending local vested interests that were seen as crucial to the stability of imperial control, for example that of the British in northern Nigeria, where they established a protectorate in 1900. There were also concerns about the economic impact of abolition. Nevertheless, slavery was ended, both by colonial policy and thanks to the slaves' attempts to seek advantage from their changing environment.

Slavery and the slave trade are understandably contentious issues. Charges of exploitation and of historic wrongs explaining present circumstances are advanced and, in some cases, contested. There is no doubt that the trade played a formative role, not only in the demographics of the Atlantic world, but also in its varied political cultures and collective memories – topics that will be briefly addressed in the last chapter.

CHAPTER 5

LEGACY AND CONCLUSIONS

Liverpool made a public apology in 1994 for its role in the slave trade, and Bristol is now under pressure to do the same. John Hawkins' descendant, Andrew, and a group of twenty friends locked themselves in chains in June 2006 in Gambia in order to demonstrate their sense of sorrow, before being forgiven by the country's Vice-President. The Church of England apologized in 2006 to the descendants of victims of the slave trade, the General Synod acknowledging the 'dehumanising and shameful' consequences of slavery. Addressing the slave experience will be thrown to the fore as we approach the bicentenary in 2007 of the prohibition of the British slave trade. The issue invites careful treatment if we are to avoid stoking ahistorical animosity.

In part, the discussion of the slave trade and slavery is an aspect of the longstanding critique of their alleged role in the development of capitalism and European power,[1] a role that critics magnify; and, in part, it is an aspect of the cult of apology that is so prominent in modern public history. It is not only Britain that is involved, as the pressure from China and Korea for an apologetic tone on the part of Japan over its imperialism and military conduct in the early twentieth century indicates; but British imperialism is a key issue in the cult of apology.

So, also, is the treatment of the black experience in the USA, with slavery serving to emphasize distinctive development, and thus challenging ideas of cultural syncretism, let alone benign American exceptionalism.[2] For example, in 2000, in response to discussion of the Interior Appropriations

Bill, the National Park Service submitted to Congress a report assessing the educational information at Civil War sites and recommending that much be updated, not least to illustrate the 'breadth of human experience during the period, and establish the relevance of the war to people today'. Representative Jesse Jackson Jr. and other members of Congress had complained that many sites lacked appropriate contextualization and, specifically, that there was often 'missing vital information about the role that the institution of slavery played in causing the American Civil War'. The treatment of the American Civil War is particularly contentious, with the issue of slavery highlighted in order to criticize antebellum Southern culture and to present the South as 'un-American' or 'anti-American'; meanwhile, in contrast, Southern apologists emphasize the rights of states.

Thus, controlling and defining the past becomes an aspect of current politics. Charges of exploitation and of historic wrongs explaining present circumstances are contested, especially in the 'white South', which has its own aggressive and self-righteous sense of historical grievance. In 1990, Virginia elected America's first black Governor, Douglas Wilder, a grandson of slaves; but, at the same time, there was considerable resistance in parts of the South, for example Mississippi, to abandoning the Confederate flag and other symbols of difference and defiance – symbols that, to critics, contributed to the intimidation of blacks. In 1998, David Beasley lost his post as Governor of South Carolina for supporting the removal of the flag from the statehouse.

This situation is exacerbated when other issues, such as gender, are involved. Thus, the charge that Thomas Jefferson had an affair with an African-American servant, Sally Hemings, led to contention in the 1990s and early 2000s, with one affronted American participant walking out of a University of Virginia Jefferson Symposium I attended in 1998. The charge was seen by some as an assault on the integrity of the Founding Fathers, while the emphasis on the relationship seems to obscure Jefferson's achievements, and is nearly always taken out of context.

There were apologies for American history. In 2005, the Senate formally apologized for neglecting to pass legislation in the late nineteenth and early twentieth centuries to make lynching a federal crime. Earlier, the contentious legacy of slavery was accentuated by controversy over civil rights, and, in turn, that provided a perspective for considering slavery and the slave trade. The assertion of African identity by some in the black rights movement is directly pertinent. William Du Bois (1868–1963), one of the founders, in 1909, of the National Association for the Advancement of Colored People, and, as a historian, the author of *The Suppression of the African Slave Trade* (1896) and the very critical *The World and Africa* (1947), emigrated in 1960 to Ghana, where he supported the idea of an *Encyclopaedia Africana*. This assertion of African identity was the case, in particular, with black separatists, but also with others who were not separatists. In his speech at Detroit on 14 February 1965, given a week before he was assassinated, Malcolm X declared:

> One of the things that made the Black Muslim movement grow was its emphasis upon things African. This was the secret to the growth of the Black Muslim movement. African blood, African origin, African culture, African ties ... we discovered that deep within the subconscious of the black man in this country, he is still more African than he is American.

Aside from African consciousness, the experience of slavery, and thus the background of the slave trade, served as a reference point to those pressing for civil rights. In his 'I have a dream' speech, delivered on the steps of the Lincoln Memorial in Washington on 28 August 1963, Martin Luther King Jr. declared that, despite the Emancipation Proclamation, 'One hundred years later, the life of the Negro is still sadly crippled by the manacles of segregation and the chains of discrimination.'

In the USA, as in Brazil, the poor, indeed, remain to this day disproportionately black, and the black disproportionately poor. The percentage of blacks below the poverty line in the USA was 35.7 in 1983, 22.5 in 2000, and 24.7 in 2004, compared to percentages for non-Hispanic whites of eight to nine. The percentage of whites in the population, however, ensured that the number of whites below the poverty line was greater than that of blacks. At the national level, in the early 2000s, black mothers were twice as likely as their white counterparts to give birth to a low-weight baby, and their children were twice as likely to die before their first birthday. Furthermore, blacks are disproportionately numerous in the prison population. In Brazil, slave-like conditions, in which debt bondage is linked to the seizure of identity papers, and to cruel treatment by armed guards, are seen today, for example in the pig-iron industry around Maraba.

As far as Britain is concerned, the process of apology was a matter of a re-evaluation of aspects of imperialism and colonialism, and the treatment of the slave trade should be approached in this context. There were calls, for example, to confront the legacy of rule over Ireland (a rule which also, in fact, divided the Irish). In 1997, Tony Blair marked the 150th anniversary of the Great Famine in Ireland by issuing a statement declaring that those 'who governed in London at the time failed their people by standing by while a crop failure turned into a massive human tragedy'. This admission of guilt was criticized by Northern Irish Unionists, committed to defending the historical legacy and memory of the Union between Britain and Ireland, as well as by conservative commentators in Britain, the *Daily Telegraph* claiming that Blair had given support to 'the self-pitying nature of Irish nationalism'. The Famine certainly plays a major role in the nationalist account of Irish history, both in Ireland and in the Irish diaspora, particularly in the USA. The Famine allegedly demonstrated that Ireland had been harshly treated when part of Britain, and therefore showed that Irish commentators who defended the link were, at best, mistaken.

It is unclear what use is served by a British apology, other than validating this tendentious account. Rowan Williams, the Archbishop of Canterbury, told the General Synod in

2006 that apology for the Church's role in the slave trade was 'necessary', adding 'The body of Christ is not just a body that exists at any one time; it exists across history and we therefore share the shame and the sinfulness of our predecessors and part of what we can do, with them and for them in the body of Christ, is prayerful acknowledgement of the failure that is part of us not just of some distant "them".' Apologies, however, all too often conform to fatuous arguments about 'closure', resolution, and being unable to move on until we acknowledge the past, whereas in practice they entail the opposite of all of these and, instead, involve the reiteration of grievance.

The British are also expected to apologize for other imperial episodes, such as the Amritsar Massacre of 1919 in India, which, indeed, at the time, led to a government inquiry and a legal case. A 1997 state visit to India by Elizabeth II proved controversial, when her husband, Philip, Duke of Edinburgh, failed to show the expected contrition over Amritsar. It is ironic that the slave trade should be seen as in particular need of apology, as Britain played the leading role in its abolition, and, despite charges of self-interest and/or hypocrisy, this was, in practice, very much an example of an ethical foreign policy. Henry, 3rd Viscount Palmerston (who had three spells as Foreign Secretary – in 1830–4, 1835–41 and 1846–51 – and two as Prime Minister) and Edward, 14th Earl of Derby (who twice occupied the office of Secretary of State for the Colonies – in 1833–4 and 1841–4 – and later also became Prime Minister) were both committed opponents of the slave trade, as was Derby's son, Edward, the 15th Earl, who was Foreign Secretary in 1866–8 and 1874–8. Much diplomatic and considerable military effort was expended by Britain on suppression of the slave trade.

Slavery and the slave trade were, and are, intertwined as issues with other aspects of public history. Abolition played an important part in French public culture, not least as a sign of republican virtue in contrast to the *ancien régime*. Thus, the Revolutionaries ended the slave trade, only for Napoleon to restore and then (at the close of his career) abolish it. As far as slavery is concerned, it was the Republic, which replaced the Orléans monarchy, that passed the Abolition Act in 1848. The continued resonance of abolitionism chimes with left-wing French thought, and it was under a Socialist government that, in 1993, the remains of Abbé Grégoire were moved into the Panthéon in Paris. The positive and large-scale contribution of African soldiers from the colonies to the defence of France and French interests in both World Wars (and more generally) helped contribute to a more positive attitude to blacks.

The lasting legacy of slavery, however, became more contentious in the 2000s, as a result of racial discontent in France, as well as controversy over the future of the colonial *Départements d'Outre-Mer*. In France and elsewhere, it has not only been progressives that have condemned the slave trade; it has also come in for criticism from, among others, racists opposed to the possibilities it offered for intermarriage and deracination. Thus, the Nazi Manfred Sell, in his *Die schwarze Völkerwanderung* (*The Black Migration*) (1940), attacked the slave trade because it led to racial mixing.[3]

The situation among former slave-trading states varied and varies. The slave trade and slavery were, for example, a less prominent issue in the Netherlands than in Britain. This is even more the case in Denmark, where they are a very minor issue. The overseas colonies never had a prominent place on the Danish political agenda or in Danish collective memory. The colonies were small, and very few Danes actually had any direct contact with them. Only a small part of the population of the Danish West Indies were Danes, most of the planters being British or Dutch, so connections with Denmark and the memories of Danish rule soon vanished. Like many Western countries today, immigration is a major issue in Denmark. However, unlike Britain or France, large numbers of immigrants do not come from areas that used to be Danish colonies, and thus there is no direct link between Denmark's colonial past and her present-day problems with immigration.

The theme of apology provides only a very partial guide to the facets, let alone the rights and wrongs, that modern observers might discuss. In particular, in the calls for apology there is an emphasis on European agency, which downplays the active role of others. In short, the demand for European apology, paradoxically, is an aspect of the very Eurocentric ranking that is frequently complained about. This focus on the Europeans leads to a failure to understand important aspects of the trade.

Instead of this approach, it is important to give due weight to African agency, and, moreover, to consider the extent to which Arabs also played a role in the 'out of Africa' trade – and went on doing so after the Europeans had ceased their role. In the 1890s, in the British Parliament there was considerable political pressure on the government over the continuing role in the slave trade of the Sultanate of Zanzibar, which was a British protectorate. The Arab role can be amplified by considering the ethnic tensions that underlie the very harsh treatment of blacks in Darfur in the 2000s, and also by discussing other episodes of slavery and slave trade in world history, whether they were *de jure* or, as more commonly in the modern world, *de facto* systems.

The Islamic world was also fed with slaves from other directions, including from Christian Europe during the Middle Ages and thereafter, as well as from Central Asia. In the fifteenth, sixteenth and seventeenth centuries, the Crimean Tatars launched large-scale slave raids on Muscovy, as in 1571. There was also a pattern of slave raiding by more nomadic societies on their more settled counterparts, and this remained the case in the nineteenth century. Uzbek slave raids on Persia in the 1860s and 1870s were a major issue for Britain and Russia as they sought to bring stability to Central Asia. When the Russians occupied the oasis of Khiva in 1873, they liberated 30,000 slaves, some of whom were Russians, although many were Persians. I am told that, even today, it is not hard to visualize the froth and bustle of the slave market in Khiva's narrow streets.

This, however, invites the reflection that Atlantic slavery was exceptional, because it led to the racism that is of lasting importance in defining white–black relations. A distinctive presentation of blackness is visible in classical Rome,[4] but the role of Atlantic slavery has been seen as much more important for recent attitudes.

If blame is to be heaped on the Europeans, however, and, even more, if wild and inappropriate talk of genocide or Holocaust is to be employed, then it is more pertinent to consider the Western impact on the Native population of the Americas in this light than the impact on Africa. Statistics are difficult to come by, but, in terms of European power projection and the percentage of the population killed as a result of European contact, the figures are far more grim for the Americas. In part, this was a result of disease, but the inroads of the latter were furthered as a consequence of the disruption caused by European conquest. This conquest proved far more disruptive, indeed total, than the later European conquest of Africa.

As for slavery and the slave trade, these were also acute issues for Natives in the early stages of European conquest of the Americas, at a period in which the trans-Atlantic slave trade was still relatively modest. Even when it became more active, slave raiding continued in the Americas, although this tends to be downplayed, because it was characteristic rather of Spanish and, even more, Portuguese America, rather than of British America, especially once the Atlantic slave trade was well developed.

Indeed, the Atlantic slave trade can be better appreciated if the more widespread and varied nature of coerced labour in the Americas is considered. This range is rather overlooked, because indentured white labour in North America was, on the whole, far less dire than slavery, not least because whites could move to the open frontier of opportunity. The situation, however, is less comfortable if the treatment of Native labour in Latin America is considered, and this underlines the mistake of isolating the Atlantic slave trade.

Such a consideration can lead to the reflection that, however brutal, slavery was like serfdom or (in a rather different way) indentured labour – a device to ensure labour availability and control. It is misleading, therefore, to treat one of these devices as uniquely in need of apology. This can be underscored if we also consider the peasant uprisings in seventeenth- and eighteenth-century Europe. The demand for apology again both simplifies the past and tells us more about the present.

The symbolic role of the slave trade as the nadir of black abasement ensures that it stands for black weakness and exploitation by others: take, for instance, the *Independent* of 13 September 2006, in which Archbishop Desmond Tutu referred to the arms trade as the new slave trade. This exploitation and victimization are seen as, at once, commodification and racism. However, an emphasis on African agency in the slave trade emerges ever more clearly as Europe's relative weakness in Africa prior to the late nineteenth century is considered. This is one of the themes of this book. It is an important point that arises from work on military history, which helps to explain why that is emphasized here. This work has not been adequately integrated with consideration of the slave trade, particularly at the public level, but any such integration makes it clear that discussion of African vulnerability is misplaced – indeed woefully so.

Instead, attention should be directed to a subject that is far more obscure, owing to the nature of the sources and the scholarship: namely, conflict between Africans. This resulted in captives, whether or not they were slaughtered or kept as slaves. If the latter, some would be retained in slavery by their captors (a subject that receives insufficient attention), and others would be sold into distant slavery, again both in Africa and further afield (entailing both the European and the Arab slave trade). Slave trading by African powers, for example in the interior of West Africa, remained large-scale well into the nineteenth century.

There is, indeed, an element of the ridiculous in some apologies, for those to whom they are made may well be the descendants of African slave traders, rather than of the enslaved, and this is especially the case along the Atlantic coast. Again, comparisons with the Holocaust are particularly inappropriate, and indeed neglect both the role of African agency and the degree to which Africans survived the travails of the trade. It is also unclear what percentage of its population Africa lost, whether it was replaced by higher rates of reproduction, and whether, irrespective of this, the creation of an African diaspora, however involuntary, should, in the long term, be regarded as a disaster.

This has been underlined more recently by the large-scale movement of Africans to Europe, particularly Spain. Most have come from West Africa, for example from Mali and Burkina Faso, in search of work in Europe. A key means of access is from Mauritania, Gambia and, particularly, Senegal, by boat to the Canary Islands, a Spanish possession, where they seek asylum. Crossing in open boats, they are exposed to the sun and are generally short of water. The boats are very crowded and a certain number die in the crossing. Others are shipwrecked. In the year from August 2005 to August 2006, 20,000 African refugees arrived in the Canaries and up to 3,000 are thought to have died. The Red Cross estimates that one boat in four sinks on a journey that may take up to ten days; from Senegal it is 950 miles.

The relationship between this and the slave trade is, at best, indirect, as the would-be migrants are not slaves. Looked at differently, however, if the emphasis is on economics, the contemporary example underlines the extent to which labour flows are not always characterized by agreeable circumstances. It also indicates that the combined pressure of demographic expansion and economic difficulties ensures that labour is now exported from Africa.

The pertinent comparison may be not to the classical Atlantic slave trade, but rather to the impact on African economies in the nineteenth century of the arrival of European goods, particularly textiles and metals – goods that, in contrast to the eighteenth century, became available in larger and cheaper quantities thanks to the economies of scale brought by the use of steamships. This hit African industries and led both to the growth of primary production focused on the European market, for example of palm oil, and also to a rise in the slave trade within Africa, one that was exploited for the last stages of the Atlantic slave trade and also for the Arab slave trade.

The sight of Africans in open boats being intercepted by the Spanish navy in an attempt to keep them from the European economy invites attention to the varied relationship between globalization and movement for work, with a coda about the different role of naval power compared to that of the nineteenth-century British navy. The current situation also underlines the continuing complexity of the relationship between Africa and the forces in the world economy.

Another instructive point arises from the savagery of warfare in Africa in the 1990s and 2000s. Although the warfare in Sudan has echoes of earlier Arab slaving, most of the warfare, particularly in Rwanda and Congo, reveals a savagery that cannot be linked to the slave trade. This point can be taken back into the period of the trade. For example, the scale and bitterness of the Mfecane wars in southern Africa, caused by the rise of the Zulu empire in the early nineteenth century and competition for resources, cannot be readily linked to the slave trade, nor indeed attributed to exogenous pressures in the shape of European actions. As with modern conflicts (for example in the provision of weaponry), such pressures did play a role, but they were instrumental rather than causative. Such an analysis of African developments is unacceptable to many, because it can be seen to be critical; but, leaving aside the point that possibly such criticism is not misplaced, that is no reason not to consider this assessment from the historical perspective.

Apology tells us more about modern sensitivities than about the past. As such, it is an aspect of the continued moulding of the past in order to provide an exemplary history for the purposes of the present. As an aspect of this, apology can provide a distinctive 'feel-good' quality. That governments have generally taken part in an appropriation of the past in order to provide an exemplary history does not mean that scholars should connive at the processes. Instead, a key aspect of history is that it provides healthy scepticism in the face of all overarching theories and ready judgments, particularly if the latter serve convenient political purposes, indeed fictions.

Slavery and the slave trade were vile. It is good that they no longer exist in the form and on the scale discussed in this book. Vile, but not unique as forms of labour control, nor as reflections of ethnic and other prejudice. Similarly, the vileness of the slave trade is not lessened by the large degree of African and Arab agency; but that serves as a reminder of the need for caution before moving from analysis to judgment. More generally, the use of a public myth of past suffering as a justification for particular political and cultural strategies is unhelpful, and indeed, in this case, part of the self-imposed impoverishment of sections of the African world and diaspora. The curse of the past lies not in what happened, but rather in the inability to look to the future. The latter should not be confronted in terms rigidly dictated by a sense of grievance, a sense that can lead to the denial of choice and the neglect of opportunities. The idea of empowerment through grievance is negative and, indeed, dangerous for all concerned. In Shakespeare's play *Romeo and Juliet*, a distraught Romeo tells Friar Lawrence, who is trying to offer reasonable counsel, 'Thou canst not speak of that thou dost not feel.' Fortunately, there are very few today who suffer the pain and humiliation of slavery. For those who do not, grievances should be indulged as little as possible.

NOTES

INTRODUCTION

1. C. A. Palmer, 'Defining and studying the modern African diaspora', *Perspectives* 36:6 (1988), pp. 22–5; B. C. McMillan (ed.), *Captive Passage: The Transatlantic Slave Trade and the Making of the Americas* (Washington, 2002).

2. J. J. Ewald, 'Slavery in Africa and the slave trades from Africa', *American Historical Review* 97 (1992), p. 466.

3. J. Thornton, 'The slave trade in eighteenth century Angola: Effects on demographic structures', *Canadian Journal of African Studies* 14 (1980), pp. 417–27.

4. R. A. Austen, *African Economic History: Internal Development and External Dependency* (Portsmouth, New Hampshire, 1987), p. 275, and 'The 19th century Islamic slave trade from East Africa: A tentative census', in W. G. Clarence-Smith (ed.), *The Economics of the Indian Ocean Slave Trade in the Nineteenth Century* (London, 1989), pp. 21–44.

5. D. A. E. Pelteret, *Slavery in Early Medieval England* (Woodbridge, 1995), pp. 251–6.

6. A. L. Poole, *From Domesday Book to Magna Carta* (Oxford, 1955), p. 40.

7. J. Guilmartin, *Gunpowder and Galleys: Changing Technology and Mediterranean Warfare at Sea in the Sixteenth Century* (Cambridge, 1974).

8. J. R. Willis (ed.), *Slaves and Slavery in Muslim Africa*. Vol. I: *Islam and the Ideology of Enslavement* (London, 1985).

9. W. S. Holdsworth, *History of English Law*, VI (London, 1924), pp. 264–5.

10. C. Vann Woodward, *American Counterpoint: Slavery and Racism in the North-South Dialogue* (Boston, 1971).

11. For the economy of serfdom, A. Kahan, *The Plow, the Hammer and the Knout: An Economic History of Eighteenth-Century Russia* (Chicago, Illinois, 1985). For slavery, R. Hellie, *Slavery in Russia, 1450–1725* (Chicago, 1982).

12. A. R. Ekrich, *Bound for America: The Transportation of British Convicts to the Colonies, 1718–1775* (Oxford, 1987); A. Smith, *An Inquiry into the Nature and Wealth of Nations* (London, 1776; Oxford edition, 1979), p. 386.

13. J. A. G. Roberts, *A History of China* (2nd edn, Basingstoke, 2006), p. 5.

14. E. D. Domar, 'The causes of slavery or serfdom: A hypothesis', *Journal of Economic History* 30 (1970), pp. 18–32; S. Engerman, 'Some considerations relating to property rights in man', *Journal of Economic History* 33 (1973), pp. 43–65.

15. R. C. Hoffmann, *Land, Liberties, and Lordship in a Late Medieval Countryside. Agrarian Structures and Change in the Duchy of Wroclaw* (Philadelphia, Pennsylvania, 1989).

16. J. Blum, *Lord and Peasant in Russia from the Ninth to the Nineteenth Century* (Princeton, 1961), and *The End of the Old Order in Rural Europe* (Princeton, 1978).

CHAPTER 1

1. H. F. Dobyns, 'Estimating Aboriginal American population: An appraisal of techniques with a new hemispheric estimate', *Current Anthropology* 7 (1966), pp. 395–449; J. D. Daniels, 'The Indian population of North America in 1492', *William and Mary Quarterly* 49 (1992), pp. 298–320.

2. A. Crosby, *The Columbian Exchange: Biological and Cultural Consequences of 1492* (Westport, Connecticut, 1969), and *Ecological Imperialism: The Biological Expansion of Europe, 1500–1900* (London, 1986).

3. F. Moya Pons, 'The Tainos of Hispaniola', *Caribbean Review* 13 (1984), pp. 20–3, 47; L. A. Newson, *Aboriginal and Spanish Colonial Trinidad: A Study in Culture Contact* (London, 1976); N. D. Cook, *Demographic Collapse: Indian Peru, 1520–1620* (Cambridge, 1981); K. Sale, *The Conquest of Paradise* (London, 1990).

4. S. A. Alchon, *A Pest in the Land: New World Epidemics in a Global Perspective* (Albuquerque, New Mexico, 2003).

5. A. M. Stevens-Arroyo, 'The inter-Atlantic paradigm: The failure of Spanish medieval colonization of the Canary and Caribbean islands', *Journal of Comparative Studies in Society and History* 35 (1993), p. 521.

6. F. Fernández-Armesto, *Before Columbus: Exploration and Colonization from the Mediterranean to the Atlantic, 1229–1492* (Philadelphia, 1987), pp. 212–13.

7. G. D. Jones, 'The last Maya frontiers of colonial Yucatán', in M. J. MacLeod and R. Wassertrom (eds), *Spaniards and Indians in Southeastern Mesoamerica: Essays on the History of Ethnic Relations* (Lincoln, Nebraska, 1983), pp. 64–91.

8. P. Powell, *Soldiers, Indians and Silver: The Northward Advance of New Spain, 1550–1600* (Berkeley, California, 1952); R. C. Padden, 'Cultural change and military resistance in Araucanian Chile, 1550–1730', *Southwestern Journal of Anthropology* (1957), pp. 103–21; P. Boucher, *Cannibal Encounters. Europeans and Island Caribs, 1492–1763* (Baltimore, Maryland, 1993). Native when capitalized from here on refers to Native Americans, descended from the pre-Iberian conquest population and not to those born in the Americas, who might include the descendants of the conquerors.

9. J. Hemming, *Red Gold: The Conquest of the Brazilian Indians, 1500–1760* (2nd edn, London, 1995), pp. 72–3, 78–9, 90–3.

10. J. M. Monteiro, 'From Indian to slave: Forced Native labour and colonial society in Sao Paulo during the seventeenth century', *Slavery and Abolition* 9 (1988), pp. 105–27.

11. R. A. Williams, *The American Indian in Western Legal Thought: The Discourses of Conquest* (New York, 1990).

12. L. B. Simpson, *The Encomienda in New Spain: The Beginning of Spanish Mexico* (3rd edn, Berkeley, California, 1966); W. L. Sherman, *Forced Native Labor in Sixteenth-Century Central America* (Lincoln, Nebraska, 1979); O. N. Bolland, 'Colonization and slavery in Central America', in P. E. Lovejoy and N. Rogers (eds), *Unfree Labour in the Development of the Atlantic World* (Ilford, 1994), pp. 11–25.

13. B. Rushforth, '"A little flesh we offer you": The origins of Indian slavery in New France', *William and Mary Quarterly* 60 (2003), pp. 777–808.

14. P. Gerhard, 'A black conquistador in Mexico', *Hispanic American Historical Review* 58 (1978), pp. 451–9; M. Restall, 'Black conquistadors: Armed Africans in early Spanish America', *The Americas* 57 (2000), pp. 171–206.

15. C. A. Palmer, *Slaves of the White God: Blacks in Mexico, 1570–1650* (Cambridge, Massachusetts, 1976), p. 28.

16. F. Bowser, *The African Slave in Colonial Peru, 1524–1650* (Stanford, California, 1974). More generally, M. J. MacLeod, *Spanish Central America: A Socioeconomic History, 1520–1720* (Berkeley, California, 1973).

17. P. Bakewell, 'Spanish America: Empire and its outcome', in J. H. Elliott (ed.), *The Hispanic World* (London, 1991), pp. 74–5.

18. P. E. Lovejoy, 'The volume of the Atlantic slave trade: A synthesis', *Journal of African History* 23 (1982), pp. 473–502.

19. S. B. Schwartz, 'Indian labor and new world plantations: European demands and Indian responses in northeastern Brazil', *American Historical Review* 81 (1978), pp. 72–3; A. Marchant, *From Barter to Slavery: The Economic Relations of Portuguese and Indians in the Settlement of Brazil, 1500–1580* (Baltimore, Maryland, 1942).

20. I. Wilks, 'Waranga, Akan and the Portuguese in the fifteenth and sixteenth centuries', *Journal of African History*, vol. 23 (1982), pp. 330–1.

21. J. Vogt, *Portuguese Rule on the Gold Coast, 1469–1682* (Athens, Georgia, 1979).

22. P. E. H. Hair, 'Protestants as pirates, slavers and proto-missionaries: Sierra Leone 1568 and 1582', *Journal of Ecclesiastical History* 21 (1970), p. 213.

23. V. Rau, 'The Madeiran sugar cane plantations', in H. B. Johnson, Jr. (ed.), *From Reconquest to Empire: The Iberian Background to Latin American History* (New York, 1970), pp. 71–84; S. M. Greenfield, 'Madeira and the beginning of new world sugar cane cultivation and plantation slavery', in V. D. Rubin and A. Tuden (eds), *Comparative Perspectives on Slavery in New World Plantation Societies* (New York, 1977), pp. 536–52.

24. L. Felipe de Alencastro, 'The apprenticeship of colonization', in B. L. Solow (ed.), *Slavery and the Rise of the Atlantic System* (Cambridge, 1991), pp. 168–9.

25. C. A. Palmer, 'From Africa to the Americas: Ethnicity in the early black communities of the Americas', *Journal of World History* 6 (1995), pp. 223–36, esp. pp. 235–6.

26. J. D. Fage, 'Slaves and society in Western Africa, *c.* 1445–*c.* 1700', *Journal of African History* 21 (1980), pp. 289–310, esp. 309–10.

27. M. Newitt, *A History of Portuguese Overseas Expansion, 1400–1668* (Abingdon, 2005), p. 45.

28. K. G. Davies, 'The living and the dead: White mortality in West Africa, 1684–1732', in S. L. Engerman and E. D. Genovese (eds), *Race and Slavery in the Western Hemisphere: Qualitative Studies* (Princeton, 1975), pp. 88–93.

29. A. W. Lawrence, *Trade Castles and Forts of West Africa* (London, 1963).

30. Gustav Ungerer, private correspondence.

31. A. J. R. Russell-Wood, 'Iberian expansion and the issue of black slavery: Changing Portuguese attitudes 1440–1700', *American Historical Review* 83 (1978), pp. 20–1.

32. R. Unwin, *The Defeat of John Hawkins* (London, 1960).

33. J. W. Blake, 'English trade with the Portuguese empire in West Africa, 1581–1629', *Quarto Congreso do Mundo Português* 6, 1 (1940), pp. 313–41; K. R. Andrews, N. P. Canny and P. E. H. Hair (eds), *The Westward Enterprise: English Activities in Ireland, the Atlantic and America, 1460–1650* (Liverpool, 1978).

34. D. Burwash, *English Merchant Shipping, 1460–1540* (Toronto, 1947); I. Friel, *The Good Ship: Ships, Shipbuilding and Technology in England, 1200–1520* (London, 1995).

35. On these risks, P. E. Pérez-Mallaína, *Spain's Men of the Sea: Daily Life on the Indies Fleets in the Sixteenth Century* (Baltimore, Maryland, 1998); C. A. Fury, *Tides in the Affairs of Men: The Social History of Elizabethan Seamen, 1580–1603* (Westport, Connecticut, 2002).

36. T. F. Earle and K. J. P. Lowe (eds), *Black Africans in Renaissance Europe* (Cambridge, 2005).

CHAPTER 2

1. R. Matthee, 'Exotic substances: The introduction and global spread of tobacco, coffee, cocoa, tea, and distilled liquor, sixteenth to eighteenth centuries', in R. Porter and M. Teich (eds), *Drugs and Narcotics in History* (Cambridge, 1995), pp. 38–46; J. Walvin, *Fruits of Empire: Exotic Produce and British Taste, 1660–1800* (London, 1997).

2. A. L. Butler, 'Europe's Indian nectar: The transatlantic cacao and chocolate trade in the seventeenth century' (M. Litt., Oxford, 1993).

3. R. J. Ferry, 'Encomienda, African slavery, and agriculture in seventeenth-century Caracas', *Hispanic American Historical Review* 61 (1981), pp. 620–36.

4. J. R. Ward, 'The profitability of sugar planting in the British West Indies, 1650–1834', *Economic History Review*, 2nd ser., 31 (1978), p. 208.

5. A. E. Smith, *Colonists in Bondage: White Servitude and Convict Labor in America, 1607–1776* (Chapel Hill, North Carolina, 1947).

6. D. Hancock (ed.), *The Letters of William Freeman, London Merchant, 1678–1685* (London, 2002), p. xl.

7. D. H. Akenson, *If the Irish Ran the World: Montserrat, 1630–1730* (Montréal, 1997).

8. H. Beckles, 'The economic origins of black slavery in the British West Indies, 1640–1680: A tentative analysis of the Barbados model', *Journal of Caribbean History* 16 (1982), pp. 36–56, esp. pp. 52–4.

9. H. Beckles, *White Slavery and Black Servitude in Barbados, 1627–1715* (Knoxville, Tennessee, 1989); L. Gragg, '"To Procure Negroes": The English slave trade to Barbados, 1627–60', *Slavery and Abolition* 16 (1995), pp. 70, 74.

10. H. Beckles and A. Downes, 'The economics of transition to the black labor system in Barbados, 1630–1680', *Journal of Interdisciplinary History* 18 (1987), pp. 246–7.

11. T. Burnard, 'Who bought slaves in early America? Purchasers of slaves from the Royal African Company in Jamaica, 1674–1708', *Slavery and Abolition* 17 (1996), p. 88.

12. E. Vila Vilar, *Hispanoamérica y el comercio de esclavos: Los asientos portugueses* (Seville, 1977).

13. C. R. Boxer, *Salvador da Sá and the Struggle for Brazil and Angola 1602–1686* (London, 1952) and *The Dutch in Brazil, 1624–1654* (Oxford, 1957).

14. G. J. Ames, 'Pedro II and the Estado da India: Braganzan absolutism and overseas empire, 1668–1683', *Luso-Brazilian Review* 34 (1997), pp. 9–10; E. Van Veen, *Decay or Defeat? An Enquiry into the Portuguese Decline in Asia, 1580–1645* (Leiden, 2000).

15. N. Zahedieh, 'Trade, plunder, and economic development in early English Jamaica, 1655–89', *Economic History Review*, 2nd ser., 39 (1980), pp. 205–22.

16. V. A. Shepherd, 'Livestock and sugar: Aspects of Jamaica's agricultural development from the late seventeenth to the early nineteenth century', *Historical Century* 34 (1991), pp. 627–43.

17. R. Law, 'The first Scottish Guinea Company, 1634–9', *Scottish Historical Review* 76 (1997), pp. 185–202.

18. R. Ollard, *Man of War: Sir Robert Holmes and the Restoration Navy* (London, 1969).

19. P. E. Lovejoy, 'The volume of the Atlantic slave trade: A synthesis', *Journal of African History* 23 (1982), p. 481.

20. A. M. Carlos and J. B. Kruse, 'The decline of the Royal African Company: Fringe firms and the role of the charter', *Economic History Review* 49 (1996), pp. 291–313; K. Morgan (ed.), *The British Transatlantic Slave Trade. II. The Royal African Company* (London, 2003).

21. D. Geggus, 'The French slave trade: An overview', *William and Mary Quarterly* 58 (2001), p. 120.

22. F. Guerra, 'The influence of disease on race, logistics and colonization in the Antilles', *Journal of Tropical Medicine and Hygiene* 69 (1966), pp. 33–5.

23. T. Burnard, '"The Countrie Continues Sicklie": White mortality in Jamaica, 1655–1780', *Social History of Medicine* 12 (1999), pp. 45–72, esp. 55–6, 71.

24. E. S. Morgan, 'The first American boom: Virginia 1618 to 1630', *William and Mary Quarterly*, 3rd ser., 28 (1971), pp. 169–98, esp. 197.

25. R. Menard, 'The tobacco industry in the Chesapeake colonies, 1617–1730: An interpretation', *Research in Economic History* 5 (1980), pp. 109–77, esp. 153–5.

26. R. Menard, 'From servants to slaves: The transformation of the Chesapeake labor system', *Southern Studies* 16 (1977), pp. 355–90, esp. p. 389.

27. R. McColley, 'Slavery in Virginia, 1619–1660: A reexamination', in R. H. Abzug and S. E. Maizlish (eds), *New Perspectives on Race and Slavery in America* (Lexington, Kentucky, 1986), pp. 11–24; J. Horn, *Adapting to a New World: English Society in the Seventeenth-Century Chesapeake* (Chapel Hill, North Carolina, 1994).

28. O. Patterson, 'Slavery and slave revolts: A socio-historical analysis of the First Maroon War, Jamaica, 1655–1740', *Social and Economic Studies* 19 (1970), pp. 289–325; M. Craton, 'The passion to exist: Slave rebellions in the British West Indies, 1650–1832', *Journal of Caribbean History* 13 (1980), p. 4; R. Price (ed.), *Maroon Societies: Rebel Slave Communities in the Americas* (2nd edn, Baltimore, Maryland, 1996).

29. M. Restall (ed.), *Beyond Black and Red: African-Native Relations in Colonial Latin America* (Albuquerque, New Mexico, 2005).

30. A. T. Vaughan, 'The origins debate: Slavery and racism in seventeenth-century Virginia', *Virginia Magazine of History and Biography* 97 (1989), p. 353.

31. R. S. Dunn, 'The English sugar islands and the founding of South Carolina', *South Carolina Historical Magazine* 72 (1971), pp. 81–93, esp. 85, 92–3.

32. R. C. Nash, 'South Carolina and the Atlantic economy in the late seventeenth and eighteenth centuries', *Economic History Review* 45 (1992), pp. 677–702.

33. W. Rodney, 'African slavery and other forms of social oppression on the Upper Guinea coast in the context of the Atlantic slave trade', *Journal of African History* 7 (1966), pp. 431–43; J. D. Fage, 'African societies and the Atlantic slave trade', *Past and Present* 125 (1989), pp. 97–115; E. W. Evans and D. Richardson, 'Hunting for rents: The economics of slaving in pre-colonial Africa', *Economic History Review*, 2nd ser., 48 (1995), pp. 665–86.

34. P. Manning, *Slavery and African Life: Occidental, Oriental and African Slave Trades* (Cambridge, 1990).

35. J. D. Fage, *Atlas of African History* (London, 1958).

36. J. Thornton, *Africa and Africans in the Making of the Atlantic World, 1400–1800* (2nd edn, Cambridge, 1998); Y. Peron, *Atlas de la Haute-Volta* (Paris, 1975), pp. 20–1; P. Pélissier, *Atlas du Sénégal* (Paris, 1980), pp. 22–5.

37. Thornton, *Africa and the Africans*, pp. 98–125, and *Warfare in Atlantic Africa, 1500–1800* (London, 1999), esp. pp. 127–39.

38. R. Law, '"Here is No Resisting the Country": The realities of power in Afro-European relations on the West African "Slave Coast"', *Itinerario* 18 (1994), pp. 50–64, esp. 52–7; W. St. Clair, *The Grand Slave Emporium: Cape Coast Castle and the British Slave Trade* (London, 2006).

39. G. Nováky, *Handelskompanier och kompanihandel. Svenska Afrikakompaniet 1649–1663* (Uppsala, 1990), English summary, pp. 241, 244.

40. R. Law and K. Mann, 'West Africa in the Atlantic community: The case of the Slave Coast', *William and Mary Quarterly* 56 (1999), pp. 307–34.

41. K. Y. Daaku, *Trade and Politics on the Gold Coast, 1600–1700* (Oxford, 1970), pp. 96–114.

42. J. Thornton, 'Warfare, slave trading and European influence: Atlantic Africa 1450–1800', in J. Black (ed.), *War in the Early Modern World* (London, 1999), p. 141.

43. E. van den Boogaart and P. C. Emmer, 'The Dutch participation in the Atlantic slave trade, 1596–1650', in H. A. Gemery and J. S. Hogendorn (eds), *The Uncommon Market: Essays in the Economic History of the Atlantic Slave Trade* (New York, 1979), p. 367; K. G. Davies, *The Royal African Company* (London, 1957), p. 292.

44. J. C. Miller, 'Some aspects of the commercial organization of slaving at Luanda, Angola, 1760–1830', in Gemery and Hogendorn (eds), *Uncommon Market*, p. 104.

45. M. Craton, *Sinews of Empire: A Short History of British Slavery* (New York, 1974), pp. 194–5.

46. S. W. Mintz and R. Price, *The Birth of African-American Culture: An Anthropological Perspective* (Boston, Massachusetts, 1976); A. J. R. Russell-Wood, *The Black Man in Slavery and Freedom in Colonial Brazil* (London, 1982); K. M. de Queirós Mattoso, *To Be a Slave in Brazil* (New Brunswick, New Jersey, 1989); C. H. Lutz, *Santiago de Guatemala, 1541–1773: City, Caste, and the Colonial Experience* (Norman, Oklahoma, 1994); R. D. Cope, *The Limits of Radical Domination: Plebeian Society in Colonial Mexico City, 1660–1720* (Madison, Wisconsin, 1994); J. Landers, *Black Society in Spanish Florida* (Urbana, Illinois, 1999); H. L. Bennett, *Africans in Colonial Mexico: Absolutism, Christianity, and Afro-Creole Consciousness, 1570–1640* (Bloomington, Indiana, 2003);

M. L. Conniff and T. J. Davis, *Africans in the Americas: A History of the Black Diaspora* (New York, 1994).
47. J. H. Elliott, *Empires of the Atlantic World. Britain and Spain in America 1492–1830* (New Haven, 2000), p. 107.
48. A. J. R. Russell-Wood, 'Black and mulatto brotherhoods in colonial Brazil: A study in collective behavior', *Hispanic American Historical Review* 54 (1974), pp. 567–602, esp. 581–2; R. C. Rath, 'African music in seventeenth-century Jamaica: Cultural transit and transmission', *William and Mary Quarterly*, 3rd ser., 50 (1993), pp. 700–26.

CHAPTER 3

1. Voltaire, *Candide* (1759), chapter 19. See J. M. Postma, *The Dutch in the Atlantic Slave Trades* (Cambridge, 1990).
2. P. E. Lovejoy, 'The volume of the Atlantic slave trade: A synthesis', *Journal of African History* 23 (1982), p. 478, but see upward revision in volume of slave exports from 1700 to 1810 by eight per cent in D. Richardson, 'Slave exports from West and West-Central Africa, 1700–1810: New estimates of volume and distribution', *Journal of African History* 30 (1989), pp. 1–22.
3. K. Banks, 'The illicit slave-trade out of Martinique, 1718–1756', in P. A. Coclanis, *The Atlantic Economy during the Seventeenth and Eighteenth Centuries: Organization, Operation, Practice, and Personnel* (Columbia, South Carolina, 2005).
4. C. A. Palmer, *Human Cargoes: The British Slave Trade to Spanish America, 1700–1739* (Urbana, Illinois, 1981).
5. R. Austen, 'Dutch trading voyages to Cameroon, 1721–1759: European documents and African history', *Annales de la Faculté des Lettres et Sciences Humaines, Université de Yaoundé* 6 (1975), pp. 5–27; J. Postma, 'A reassessment of the Dutch Atlantic slave trade', in J. Postma and V. Enthoven (eds), *Riches from Atlantic Commerce: Dutch Transatlantic Trade and Shipping, 1585–1817* (Leiden, 2003), p. 137.
6. R. Ross, *Cape of Torment: Slavery and Resistance in South Africa* (London, 1983).
7. S. E. Green-Pedersen, 'The history of the Danish Negro slave trade, 1733–1807', *Revue française d'histoire d'outre-mer* 62 (1975), p. 209 and 'The scope and structure of the Danish Negro slave trade', *Scandinavian Economic History Review* 19 (1971), pp. 149–97.
8. P. D. Curtin, *The Atlantic Slave Trade: A Census* (Madison, Wisconsin, 1969).
9. R. Stein, 'Measuring the French slave trade, 1713–1792/3', *Journal of African History* 19 (1978), pp. 520–1.
10. R. Stein, 'The French sugar business in the eighteenth century: A quantitative study', *Journal of Business History* 22 (1980), p. 14.
11. J. Dupâquier (ed.), *Histoire de la population française, II: De la Renaissance à 1789* (Paris, 1988), pp. 127–8; G. Martin, *Nanteau XVIIIe siècle: L'ère des négriers, 1714–1774* (Paris, 1931); H. Robert, 'Les traffics coloniaux du port de La Rochelle au XVIIIe siècle, 1713–1789', *Bulletin de la Société des Antiquaires de l'Ouest* (1949), pp. 135–79; J. Tarrade, *Le commerce colonial de la France à la fin de l'Ancien Régime* (Paris, 1972), II, p. 759; P. Butel, *Les négociations bordelais, l'Europe et les Iles au XVIIIe siècle* (Paris, 1974);

G. Debien, *Les Esclaves aux Antilles Française: XVII–XVIII siècle* (Basse-Terre, Guadeloupe, 1974); R. L. Stein, *The French Slave Trade in the Eighteenth Century: An Old Regime Business* (Madison, Wisconsin, 1979); W. B. Cohen, *The French Encounter with Africans: White Response to Blacks, 1530–1888* (Bloomington, Indiana, 1980); E. Saugéra, *Bordeaux port négrier. XVIIIe–XIXe siècles. Chronologie, économie, idéologie* (Paris, 1995); A. Roman, *Saint-Malo au temps des négriers* (Paris, 2001).

12. E. Alpers, 'The French slave trade in East Africa, 1721–1810', *Cahiers d'Études Africaines* 37 (1970), pp. 80–124.

13. C. Shammas, 'The eighteenth-century English diet and economic change', *Explorations in Economic History* 21 (1984), pp. 254–69.

14. Evelyn journal, London, British Library, Evelyn papers, vol. 49 fol. 37; NA. SP. 89/59 fol. 115.

15. T. Burnard, '"Prodigious Riches": The wealth of Jamaica before the American revolution', *Economic History Review* 54 (2001), pp. 506–24.

16. E. Piñero, 'The cacao economy of the eighteenth-century province of Caracas and the Spanish cacao market', *Hispanic American Historical Review* 68 (1988), p. 92.

17. D. J. Hamilton, *Scotland, the Caribbean and the Atlantic World 1750–1820* (Manchester, 2005), p.181.

18. R. B. Sheridan, 'The Molasses Act and the market strategy of the British sugar planters', *Journal of Economic History* 17 (1957), pp. 62–83; A. J. O'Shaughnessy, 'The formation of a commercial lobby: The West India interest, British colonial policy and the American Revolution', *Historical Journal* 40 (1997), pp. 71–95.

19. C. C. Goslinga, *The Dutch in the Caribbean and in the Guianas 1680–1791* (Assen, 1985).

20. African Company memoranda, 13, 28 Feb., 4, 18 Dec. 1724, 18 Mar. 1725, 18 Mar. 1726, Charles, 2nd Viscount Townshend, Secretary of State for the Northern Department, to William Finch, envoy in The Hague, 10 June 1726, African Company to Burchett, Secretary of the Admiralty, 28 May, 6 June, 3 Aug. 1728, NA. SP. 35/48, 54, 55, 61, 84/290, ADM 1/3810; James, Lord Waldegrave, envoy in Paris, to Thomas, Duke of Newcastle, Secretary of State for the Southern Department, 29 Mar. 1733, BL. Add. 32781; Couraud to Waldegrave, 25 June 1733, enclosing 'Observations relating to the Gum Trade', Chewton; Waldegrave papers, Chavigny, French envoy in London, to Chauvelin, French Foreign Minister, 24 Dec. 1735, AE. CP. Ang. 392; Sir Charles Wager, First Lord of the Admiralty, to Newcastle, 18 Nov. 1736, Amelot, French envoy in London, to Cambis, French Foreign Minister, 16 Feb. 1738, NA. SP. 42/21, 107/21.

21. Memorandum, 14 Aug., Evan Nepean to William Fraser, 18 Aug. 1784, NA. FO. 27/12 fols 262–4.

22. Robert Walpole, envoy in Lisbon, to William, Lord Grenville, Foreign Secretary, 13 July, 13 Aug., Grenville to Walpole, 28 June 1791, NA. FO. 63/14; Cabinet minute, 28 July 1791, BL. Add. 59306 fol. 3.

23. BL. Add. 36797 fol. 1.

24. M. Pelletier, 'La Martinique et La Guadeloupe au lendemain du Traité de Paris, l'oeuvre des ingénieurs géographes', *Chronique d'histoire maritime* 9 (1984), pp. 22–30.

25. A. J. O'Shaughnessy, *An Empire Divided. The American Revolution and the British Caribbean* (Philadelphia, Pennsylvania, 2000), p. 166.

26. L. W. Bergad, *Slavery and the Demographic and Economic History of Minas Gerais, 1720–1888* (Cambridge, 1999).

27. NA. SP. 89/30 fol. 164.

28. P. Vergier, *Flux et reflux de la traite des nègres entre le golfe de Benin et Bahia de Todos os Santos du 17e et 18e siècles* (The Hague, 1968).

29. S. B. Schwartz, *Sugar Plantations in the Formation of Brazilian Society: Bahia, 1550–1835* (Cambridge, 1985), p. 182.

30. J. C. Miller, *Way of Death: Merchant Capitalism and the Angolan Slave Trade, 1730–1830* (Madison, Wisconsin, 1988), and 'A marginal institution on the margin of the Atlantic system: The Portuguese southern Atlantic trade in the eighteenth century', in B. L. Solow (ed.), *Slavery and the Rise of the Atlantic System* (Cambridge, 1991), pp. 120–50; P. Mark, *'Portuguese' Style and Luso-African Identity: Precolonial Senegambia, Sixteenth–Nineteenth Centuries* (Bloomington, Indiana, 2002).

31. D. Sweet, 'Native resistance in eighteenth-century Amazonia: The "Abominable Muras" in war and peace', *Radical History Review* 53 (1992), p. 58.

32. J. R. Booker, 'Needed but unwanted: Black militiamen in Veracruz, Mexico, 1760–1810', *Historian* 55 (1993), p. 259; R. J. Singh, *French Diplomacy in the Caribbean and the American Revolution* (Hicksville, New York, 1977), p. 122; K. Maxwell, *Pombal. Paradox of the Enlightenment* (Cambridge, 1995), p. 120.

33. D. Richardson, 'The eighteenth-century British slave trade: Estimates of its volume and coastal distribution in Africa', *Research in Economic History* 12 (1989), pp. 151–196.

34. D. Richardson (ed.), *Bristol, Africa and the Eighteenth-Century Slave Trade to America*, II, *The Years of Ascendancy, 1730–1745* (Gloucester, 1987).

35. D. Richardson, 'The British empire and the Atlantic slave trade, 1660–1807', in P. J. Marshall (ed.), *The Oxford History of the British Empire*, II, *The Eighteenth Century* (Oxford, 1998), p. 446; J. E. Inikori, *Africans and the Industrial Revolution in England: A Study in International Trade and Economic Development* (Cambridge, 2002), esp. pp. 479–82.

36. Richardson, 'The British empire', p. 442; D. Richardson and M. M. Schofield, 'Whitehaven and the eighteenth-century British slave trade', *Transactions of the Cumberland and Westmorland Antiquarian and Archaeological Society* 102 (1992), pp. 183–204, esp. p. 195.

37. For the French equivalent, R. Lemesle, *Le commerce colonial triangulaire: XVIIIe–XIXe siècles* (Paris, 1998).

38. R. B. Sheridan, 'The commercial and financial organization of the British slave trade, 1750–1807', *Economic History Review*, 2nd ser., 11 (1958–9), pp. 249–63, esp. p. 263; J. A. Rawley, *London: Metropolis of the Slave Trade* (Columbia, Missouri, 2003).

39. N. Tatterfield, *The Forgotten Trade, Comprising the Log of the Daniel and Henry of 1700 and Accounts of the Slave Trade from the Minor Ports of England, 1698–1725* (London, 1991); M. Elder, *The Slave Trade and the Economic Development of Eighteenth-Century Lancaster* (Preston, 1992).

40. J. Clark, *La Rochelle and the Atlantic Economy during the Eighteenth Century* (London, 1982).

41. G. Daudin, 'Comment calculer les profits de la traite', *Outre-Mers: Revue d'histoire* 89 (2002), pp. 43–62 and 'Profitability of slave and long-distance trading in context: The case of eighteenth-century France', *Journal of Economic History* 64 (2004), pp. 144–71.

42. G. M. Ostrander, 'The making of the triangular trade myth', *William and Mary Quarterly* 30 (1973), pp. 635–44; J. Coughtry, *The Notorious Triangle: Rhode Island and the African Slave Trade, 1700–1807* (Philadelphia, Pennsylvania, 1981); A. Jones, 'The Rhode Island slave trade: A trading advantage in Africa', *Slavery and Abolition* 2 (1981), pp. 225–44.

43. D. Eltis and S. L. Engerman, 'Fluctuations in age and sex ratios in the transatlantic slave trade, 1663–1864', *Economic History Review*, 2nd ser., 46 (1993), p. 321.

44. J. E. Inikori, 'Market structure and the profits of the British African trade in the late eighteenth century', *Journal of Economic History* 41 (1981), pp. 745–76, esp. pp. 774–5. For the argument that there was a reasonable rate of return, W. Darity, Jr., 'Profitability of the British trade in slaves once again', *Explorations in Economic History* 26 (1989), pp. 380–4. A clear summary is offered by K. Morgan, *Slavery, Atlantic Trade and the British Economy, 1660–1800* (Cambridge, 2000), pp. 36–48.

45. W. Minchinton, 'Characteristics of British slaving vessels, 1698–1775', *Journal of Interdisciplinary History* 20 (1989), pp. 53–81, esp. p. 74.

46. J. C. Appleby, '"A Business of Much Difficulty": A London slaving venture, 1651–1654', *The Mariner's Mirror* 71, 1 (1995), pp. 3–14; A. Yacou, *Journaux de bord et de traite de Joseph Crassous de Médeuil: de La Rochelle à la côte de Guinée et aux Antilles, 1772–1776* (Paris, 2001); R. Harris, *The Diligent: A Voyage through the Worlds of the Slave Trade* (New York, 2002), re a French ship that, in 1731–2, sailed from Vannes to Africa and then Martinique before returning to Vannes; R. Damon, *Joseph Crassous de Médeuil: 1741–1793, marchand, officier de la Marine royale et négrier* (Paris, 2004).

47. H. S. Klein and S. L. Engerman, 'Slave mortality on British ships, 1791–1797', in R. Anstey and P. E. H. Hair (eds), *Liverpool, the African Slave Trade and Abolition* (Liverpool, 1976), pp. 113–25.

48. S. D. Behrendt, 'The captains in the British slave trade from 1785 to 1807', *Transactions of the Historic Society of Lancashire and Cheshire* 140 (1991), p. 115; C. M. MacInnes, *Bristol and the Slave Trade* (Bristol, 1963), pp. 10–11.

49. R. L. Roberts, *Warriors, Merchants, and Slaves: The State And The Economy In The Middle Niger Valley, 1700–1914* (Stanford, 1987); S. P. Reyna, *Wars Without End: The Political Economy of a Precolonial African State* (Hanover, New Hampshire, 1990).

50. J. Thornton, *The Kingdom of Kongo: Civil War and Transition, 1641–1718* (Madison, Wisconsin, 1983).

51. J. K. Fynn, *Asante and its Neighbours, 1700–1807* (London, 1971); R. A. Kea, 'Firearms and warfare on the Gold and Slave Coasts from the sixteenth to the nineteenth centuries', *Journal of African History* 12 (1971), pp. 185–213.

52. J. C. Miller, 'Worlds apart: Africans' encounters and Africa's encounters with the Atlantic in Angola, before 1800', *Actas do Seminário Encontro de Povos e Culturas em Angola* (1995), p. 274; D. Richardson, 'Prices of slaves in West and West-Central Africa: Toward an annual series, 1698–1807', *Bulletin of Economic Research* 43 (1991), pp. 21–56, esp. p. 47.

53. D. Eltis and D. Richardson, 'Productivity in the transatlantic slave trade', *Explorations in Economic History* 32 (1995), pp. 465–84, esp. p. 480; H. A. Gemery, J. S. Hogendorn, and M. Johnson, 'Evidence on English–African terms of trade in the eighteenth century', *Explorations in Economic History* 27 (1990), pp. 157–78, esp. p. 170.

54. J. E. Inikori, 'The import of firearms into West Africa', *Journal of African History* 18 (1977), pp. 339–68; W. Richards, 'The import of firearms into West Africa in the eighteenth century', *Journal of African History* 21 (1980), pp. 43–59; R. S. Smith, *Warfare and Diplomacy in Pre-Colonial West Africa* (2nd edn, London, 1989).

55. R. Law, 'Warfare on the West Africa Slave Coast, 1650–1850', in R. B. Ferguson and N. L. Whitehead (eds), *War in the Tribal Zone: Expanding States and Indigenous Warfare* (Santa Fé, 1992), pp. 103–26, and '"Here is No Resisting the Country". The realities of power in Afro-European relations on the West African "Slave Coast"', *Itinerario* 18 (1994), pp. 55–6.

56. J. P. Smaldone, *Warfare in the Sokoto Caliphate* (Cambridge, 1977); R. Law, *The Oyo Empire c. 1600–c. 1836: A West African Imperialism in the Era of the Atlantic Slave Trade* (Oxford, 1977), *The Horse in West African History: The Role of the Horse in the Societies of Pre-Colonial West Africa* (London, 1980), and 'The horse in pre-colonial West Africa', in G. Pezzoli (ed.), *Cavalieri dell'Africa* (Milan, 1995), pp. 175–84.

57. G. Cornwallis-West, *The Life and Letters of Admiral Cornwallis* (London, 1927), pp. 50–1.

58. D. Hancock, 'Scots in the slave trade', in N. C. Landsman (ed.), *Nation and Province in the First British Empire. Scotland and the Americas, 1600–1800* (Cranbury, New Jersey, 2001), p. 74; R. Law, 'King Agaja of Dahomey, the slave trade, and the question of West African plantations: The mission of Bulfinch Lambe and Adomo Tomo to England, 1726–32', *Journal of Imperial and Commonwealth History* 19 (1991), pp. 138–63.

59. P. E. Lovejoy and D. Richardson, 'Trust, pawnship and Atlantic history: The institutional foundations of the old Calabar slave trade', *American Historical Review* 104 (1999), pp. 333–55.

60. G. E. Brooks, *Eurafricans in Western Africa: Commerce, Social Status, Gender, and Religious Observance from the Sixteenth to the Eighteenth Century* (Oxford, 2003).

61. J. F. Searing, *West African Slavery and Atlantic Commerce. The Senegal River Valley, 1700–1860* (Cambridge, 1993); D. R. Wright, *The World and a Very Small Place in Africa* (Armonk, New York, 1997).

62. S. A. Diouf (ed.), *Fighting the Slave Trade: West African Strategies* (Athens, Ohio, 2003).

63. M. Mullin, *Africa in America: Slave Acculturation and Resistance in the American South and the British Caribbean, 1736–1831* (Urbana, Illinois, 1994).

64. S. J. Hornsby, *British Atlantic, American Frontier. Spaces of Power in Early Modern British America* (Lebanon, New Hampshire, 2005), p. 193.

65. R. R. Rea, 'Urban problems and responses in British Pensacola', *Gulf Coast Historical Review* 3 (1987), p. 56.

66. D. R. Egerton, *Gabriel's Rebellion: The Virginia Slave Conspiracies of 1800 and 1802* (Chapel Hill, North Carolina, 1997); J. Sidbury, *Ploughshares into Swords: Race, Rebellion, and Identity in Gabriel's Virginia, 1730–1810* (Cambridge, 1997).

67. H. L. Root, *Peasants and King in Burgundy: Agrarian Foundations of French Absolutism* (Berkeley, California, 1987); W. te Brake, *Shaping History. Ordinary People in European Politics, 1500–1700* (Berkeley, California, 1998); H. Beckles and K. Watson, 'Social protest and labour bargaining: The changing nature of slaves' responses to plantation life in eighteenth-century Barbados', *Slavery and Abolition* 8 (1987), pp. 272–93, esp. p. 275.

68. R. Soulodre-La France, 'Socially not so dead! Slave identities in Bourbon Nueva Granada', *Colonial Latin American Review* 10, 1 (2001), pp. 87–103; A. A. Sio, 'Marginality and free colored identity in Caribbean slave society', *Slavery and Abolition* 8 (1987), pp. 166–82.

69. P. D. Morgan, *Slave Counterpoint: Black Culture in the Eighteenth-Century Chesapeake and Lowcountry* (Chapel Hill, North Carolina, 1998).

70. T. Burnard, *Mastery, Tyranny, and Desire: Thomas Thistlewood and His Slaves in the Anglo-Jamaican World* (Chapel Hill, North Carolina, 2004); R. B. Sheridan, 'The condition of the slaves in the settlement and economic development of the British Windward Islands, 1763–1775', *Journal of Caribbean History* 24 (1990), pp. 121–45, esp. pp. 141–2; K. Mason, 'The world an absentee planter and his slaves made: Sir William Stapleton and his Nevis sugar estate, 1722–1740', *Bulletin of the John Rylands University Library of Manchester* 75 (1993), pp. 103–31, esp. p. 131. See also H. S. Klein, *Slavery in the Americas: A Comparative Study of Virginia and Cuba* (Chicago, Illinois, 1967).

71. J. E. Chaplin, *An Anxious Pursuit. Agricultural Innovation and Modernity in the Lower South, 1730–1815* (Chapel Hill, North Carolina, 1993).

72. D. H. Usner, *Indians, Settlers and Slaves in a Frontier Exchange Economy. The Lower Mississippi Valley before 1783* (Chapel Hill, North Carolina, 1992).

73. G. S. Rousseau, 'Le Cat and the physiology of Negroes', *Studies in Eighteenth-Century Culture* (1973), pp. 369–86.

74. F. Felsenstein (ed.), *English Trader, Indian Maid: Representing Gender, Race, and Slavery in the New World. An Inkle and Yarico Reader* (Baltimore, Maryland, 1999).

75. J. R. Hertzler, 'Slavery in the yearly sermons before the Georgia trustees', *Georgia Historical Quarterly*, 59 (1975), pp. 118–26.

76. Cited in D. Dabydeen, 'References to blacks in William Hogarth's *Analysis of Beauty*', *British Journal for Eighteenth-Century Studies* 5 (1982), p. 93.

77. G. W. Mullin, 'Rethinking American Negro slavery from the vantage point of the colonial era', *Louisiana Studies* 12 (1973), pp. 398–422; S. S. Hughes, 'Slaves for hire: The allocation of black labor in Elizabeth City County, Virginia, 1782 to 1810', *William and Mary Quarterly* 35 (1978), pp. 260–86.

78. B. M. Saunderson, 'The *Encyclopédie* and colonial slavery', *British Journal for Eighteenth-Century Studies* 7 (1984), pp. 15–37, esp. p. 37.

79. H. J. Lüsebrink and M. Tietz (eds), *Lectures de Raynal. L'Histoire des deux Indes en Europe et en Amérique au XVIIIe siècle* (Oxford, 1991).

80. Silhouette to Amelot, 7 Sept. 1741, NA. SP. 107/49.

81. W. T. Hutchinson *et al.* (eds), *The Papers of James Madison* (Chicago, 1962), pp. 129–30, 153; G. S. McCowen, *The British Occupation of Charleston, 1780–1782* (Columbia, South Carolina, 1972), p. 99.

82. A. A. Lawrence, *Storm over Savannah* (Athens, Georgia, 1951), p. 73.

83. B. Quarles, *The Negro in the American Revolution* (Chapel Hill, North Carolina, 1961); McCowen, *Charleston*, pp. 100–3.

84. W. Cobbett (ed.), *Parliamentary History of England from...1066 to...1803* (36 vols, London, 1806–20), vol. 20, columns 1061–2.

85. M. Mullin, 'British Caribbean and North American slaves in an era of war and revolution, 1775–1807', in J. J. Crow and L. E. Tise (eds), *The Southern Experience in the American Revolution* (Chapel Hill, North Carolina, 1978), pp. 235, 240–1.

86. A. Zilversmit, *The First Emancipation: The Abolition of Slavery in the North* (Chicago, 1967).
87. A. Walker, *Ideas Suggested on the Spot in a Late Excursion* (London, 1790), p. 108.
88. R. A. Austen and W. D. Smith, 'Private tooth decay as public economic virtue: The slave–sugar triangle, consumerism, and European industrialization', *Social Science History* 14 (1990), pp. 95–115.
89. D. Armitage and M. J. Braddick (eds), *The British Atlantic World, 1500–1800* (Basingstoke, 2002), p. 247. See also E. Mancke and C. Shammas (eds), *The Creation of the British Atlantic World* (Baltimore, Maryland, 2005).

CHAPTER 4

1. E. Gøbel, 'The Danish edict of 16th March 1792 to abolish the slave trade', in J. Parmentier and S. Spanoghe (eds), *Orbis et orbem. Liber amicorum Jan Everaert* (Ghent, 2001), pp. 251–63; S. E. Green-Pedersen, 'The economic considerations behind the abolition of the Danish Negro slave trade', in H. A. Gemery and J. S. Hogendorn (eds), *The Uncommon Market. Essays in the Economic History of the Atlantic Slave Trade* (New York, 1979), pp. 399–418. More generally, see D. Eltis and J. Walvin (eds), *The Abolition of the Atlantic Slave Trade: Origins and Effects in Europe, Africa, and the Americas* (Madison, Wisconsin, 1981).
2. A. Sens, 'Dutch anti-slavery attitudes in a decline-ridden society, 1750–1815', in G. Oostindie (ed.), *Fifty Years Later. Anti-slavery, Capitalism and Modernity in the Dutch Orbit* (Leiden, 1995), and 'Dutch debates on overseas man and his world, 1770–1820', in B. Moore and H. van Nierop (eds), *Colonial Empires Compared. Britain and the Netherlands, 1750–1850* (Aldershot, 2003), pp. 86–7.
3. P. J. Marshall, *The Making and Unmaking of Empires. Britain, India, and America c. 1750–1783* (Oxford, 2005), p. 195.
4. M. Postlethwayt, *Universal Dictionary* (4th edn, 2 vols, London, 1774), I, no pagination, entry for Africa.
5. Library of Congress, Washington, British caricature collection 2-575.
6. R. E. Close, 'Toleration and its limits in the late Hanoverian empire: The Cape Colony 1795–1828', in S. Taylor, R. Connors and C. Jones (eds), *Hanoverian Britain and Empire* (Woodbridge, 1998), p. 303.
7. D. P. Resnick, 'The Société des Amis des Noirs and the abolition of slavery', *French Historical Studies* (1972), pp. 558–69; M. Dorigny and B. Gainot, *La Société des Amis des Noirs, 1788–1799. Contributions à l'histoire de l'abolition de l'esclavage* (Paris, 1998).
8. *Archives parlementaires de 1790 à 1860: Recueil complet des débats législatifs et politiques des chambers françaises* (127 vols, Paris, 1879–1913), vol. 37, p. 152.
9. D. Geggus, 'Racial equality, slavery and colonial secession during the Constituent Assembly', *American Historical Review* (1989), pp. 1290–1308; J. J. Pierce, 'The struggle for black liberty: Revolution and emancipation in Saint Domingue', *Consortium on Revolutionary Europe. Selected Papers, 1997*, pp. 168–79.
10. C. Fink, *The Making of Haiti: The Saint Domingue Revolution from Below* (Knoxville, Tennessee, 1991).

11. R. N. Buckley, *Slaves in Red Coats: The British West India Regiments, 1795–1815* (New Haven, Connecticut, 1979).

12. B. Marshall, 'Slave resistance and white reaction in the British Windward Islands, 1763–1833', *Caribbean Quarterly* 28, no. 3 (1982), pp. 39–40.

13. W. B. Cohen, *The French Encounter with Africans: White Response to Blacks, 1530–1880* (Bloomington, Indiana, 1980), p. 119.

14. K. R. Maxwell, *Conflicts and Conspiracies: Brazil and Portugal, 1750–1808* (Cambridge, 1973), p. 222.

15. D. Turley, *The Culture of English Antislavery, 1780–1860* (London, 1991); C. Midgley, *Women Against Slavery: The British Campaigns, 1780–1870* (London, 1992).

16. E. Williams, *Capitalism and Slavery* (Chapel Hill, North Carolina, 1944). An influential work, particularly thanks to its reissues in 1961, 1964 and 1966.

17. S. H. H. Carrington, 'The state of the debate on the role of capitalism in the ending of the slave system', *Journal of Caribbean History* 22 (1988), pp. 20–41; 'British West Indian economic decline and abolition, 1775–1807: Revisiting econocide', *Canadian Journal of Latin American and Caribbean Studies* 14 (1989), pp. 33–59, and *The Sugar Industry and the Abolition of the Slave Trade, 1775–1810* (Gainesville, Florida, 2002).

18. S. Drescher, *Econocide: British Slavery in the Era of Abolition* (London, 1977).

19. J. R. Ward, 'The amelioration of British West Indian slavery, 1750–1834: Technical change and the plough', *Nieuwe West-Indische Gids* 63 (1989), pp. 43, 52, and *British West Indian Slavery, 1750–1834: The Process of Amelioration* (London, 1988).

20. R. Anstey, 'Capitalism and slavery: A critique', *Economic History Review*, 2nd ser., 21, no. 2 (1968), p. 320.

21. S. Drescher, 'Whose abolition? Popular pressure and the ending of the British slave trade', *Past and Present* 143 (1994), pp. 136–66, esp. 165–6.

22. K. Jacoby, 'Slaves by nature? Domestic animals and human slaves', *Slavery and Abolition* 15 (1994), pp. 96–7.

23. R. Anstey, *The Atlantic Slave Trade and British Abolition, 1760–1810* (London, 1975); B. Fladeland, 'Abolitionist pressures on the Concert of Europe, 1814–1832', *Journal of Modern History* 38 (1966), pp. 355–73.

24. A. Burton, 'British Evangelicals, economic warfare and the abolition of the Atlantic slave trade, 1794–1810', *Anglican and Episcopal History* 65 (1996), pp. 197–225, esp. p. 223.

25. C. J. Bartlett and G. A. Smith, 'A "Species of Milito-Nautico-Guerrilla-Plundering Warfare". Admiral Alexander Cochrane's naval campaign against the United States, 1814–1815', in J. Flavell and S. Conway (eds), *Britain and America Go to War. The Impact of War and Warfare in Anglo-America, 1754–1815* (Gainesville, Florida, 2004), pp. 187–90; John Harriott to Sidmouth, 7 May 1814, Exeter, Devon Record Office, Sidmouth papers, 152M/C1814/OF13. See also 152M/C1813/OF3 and London, National Archives, War Office papers 1/141, pp. 63–7.

26. D. Eltis, 'The British trans-Atlantic slave trade after 1807', *Journal of Maritime History* 4 (1974), pp. 1–11, and 'The British contribution to the nineteenth-century transatlantic slave trade', *Economic History Review*, 2nd ser., 32 (1979), pp. 211–27.

27. L. C. Jennings, 'French policy towards trading with African and Brazilian slave merchants', *Journal of African History* 17 (1976), pp. 515–28.

28. H. Klein and S. Engerman, 'Shipping patterns and mortality in the African slave trade to Rio de Janeiro, 1825–1830', *Cahiers d'études africaines* 15 (1975), pp. 385–7.

29. P. E. Lovejoy, 'The volume of the Atlantic slave trade: A synthesis', *Journal of African History* 23 (1982), p. 490.

30. R. J. Reid, *Political Power in Pre-Colonial Buganda: Economy, Society and Warfare in the Nineteenth-Century* (London, 2002).

31. K. O. Dike, *Trade and Politics in the Niger Delta 1830–1885* (Oxford, 1956), pp. 68–9.

32. C. A. Bayly, *The Birth of the Modern World 1780–1914. Global Connections and Comparisons* (Oxford, 2004), pp. 404–5.

33. J. C. Dorsey, *Slave Traffic in the Age of Abolition: Puerto Rico, West Africa, and the Non-Hispanic Caribbean, 1815–1859* (Gainesville, Florida, 2003).

34. M. Tadman, *Speculators and Slaves: Masters, Traders, and Slaves in the Old South* (Madison, Wisconsin, 1996); W. Johnson, *Soul By Soul: Life inside the Antebellum Slave Market* (Cambridge, Massachusetts, 1999); J. D. Martin, *Divided Mastery. Slave Hiring in the American South* (Cambridge, Massachusetts, 2004).

35. C. O. Paullin, *Atlas of the Historical Geography of the United States* (Washington, 1932); D. B. Dodd, *Historical Atlas of Alabama* (Tuscaloosa, 1974); R. D. Gastil, *Culture Regions of the United States* (Seattle, 1975).

36. W. L. Mathieson, *Great Britain and the Slave Trade, 1839–65* (London, 1929).

37. R. Conrad, 'The contraband slave trade to Brazil, 1831–1845', *Hispanic American Historical Review* 49 (1969), pp. 618–38, esp. 618–19, and *World of Sorrow: The African Slave Trade to Brazil* (Baton Rouge, Louisiana, 1986).

38. L. Bethell, *The Abolition of the Brazilian Slave Trade* (Cambridge, 1970).

39. A. F. Corwin, *Spain and the Abolition of Slavery in Cuba, 1817–1886* (Austin, Texas, 1967); D. R. Murray, *Odious Commerce: Britain, Spain and the Abolition of the Cuban Slave Trade* (Cambridge, 1980).

40. P. M. Kielstra, *The Politics of Slave Trade Suppression in Britain and France, 1814–48: Diplomacy, Morality and Economics* (Basingstoke, 2000).

41. C. N. Parkinson, *Edward Pellew, Viscount Exmouth, Admiral of the Red* (London, 1934), pp. 419–72.

42. D. Northrup, 'The compatibility of the slave and palm oil trades in the Bight of Biafra', *Journal of African History* 17 (1976), p. 357.

43. Dike, *Trade and Politics*; A. A. Boahen, *Britain, the Sahara and the Western Sudan, 1788–1861* (Oxford, 1964).

44. Stevenson to Liverpool, 1 Feb. 1812, Exeter, Devon County Record Office, 152H/C1812/OF27.

45. N. Thompson, *Earl Bathurst and the British Empire* (Barnsley, 1999), pp. 167–8.

46. J. J. Ewald, *Soldiers, Traders and Slaves: State Formation and Economic Transformation in the Greater Nile Valley, 1700–1885* (Madison, Wisconsin, 1990).

47. D. Robinson, *The Holy War of Umar Tel. The Western Sudan in the Mid-Nineteenth Century* (Oxford, 1985), p. 330.

48. C. I. Wilks, *Asante in the Nineteenth Century* (Cambridge, 1975).

49. M. Crowder and S. Miers, 'The politics of slavery in Bechuanaland: Power struggles and the plight of the Basarwa ...', in Miers and R. Roberts (eds), *The End of Slavery in Africa* (Madison, Wisconsin, 1988), pp. 175–6.

50. J. Lean and T. Burnard, 'Hearing slave voices: The Fiscal's reports of Berbice and Demerara-Essequebo', *Archives* 27 (2002), pp. 122.

51. A. J. Barker, *Slavery and Antislavery in Mauritius, 1810–33: The Conflict between Economic Expansion and Humanitarian Reform under British Rule* (London, 1996); B. W. Higman, *Slave Populations of the British Caribbean, 1807–1834* (Baltimore, Maryland, 1984).

52. M. Turner, *Slaves and Missionaries: The Disintegration of Jamaican Slave Society, 1787–1834* (Urbana, Illinois, 1982); E. V. d'Costa, *Crowns of Glory, Tears of Blood: The Demerara Slave Rebellion of 1823* (New York, 1994).

53. J. D. Milligan, 'Slave rebelliousness and the Florida Maroon', *Prologue* 6 (Spring 1974), pp. 4–18.

54. J. J. Reis, *Slave Rebellion in Brazil: The Muslim Uprising of 1835 in Bahia* (Baltimore, Maryland, 1993).

55. M. C. Karasch, *Slave Life in Rio de Janeiro, 1808–1850* (Princeton, New Jersey, 1987); B. J. Barickman, *A Bahian Counterpoint: Sugar, Tobacco, Cassava, and Slavery in the Recôncavo, 1780–1860* (Stanford, California, 1998).

56. I. Gross, 'The abolition of Negro slavery and British parliamentary politics, 1832–3', *Historical Journal* 23 (1980), p. 84.

57. S. Drescher, *From Slavery to Freedom: Comparative Studies in the Rise and Fall of Atlantic Slavery* (New York, 1999).

58. L. Dubois, 'The road to 1848: Interpreting French anti-slavery', *Slavery and Abolition* 22 (2001), pp. 150–7.

59. S. Drescher, 'Brazilian abolition in comparative perspective', *Hispanic American Historical Review* 68 (1988), p. 433.

60. R. B. Toplin, 'Upheaval, violence, and the abolition of slavery in Brazil: The case of Sao Paulo', *Hispanic American Historical Review* 49 (1969), pp. 637–39, and *The Abolition of Slavery in Brazil* (New York, 1972); R. Conrad, *The Destruction of Brazilian Slavery, 1850–1888* (Berkeley, California, 1972); H. Clementi, *La abolición de la esclavitud en América Latina* (Buenos Aires, 1974); P. A. Howard, *Changing History: Afro-Cuban Cabildos and Societies of Color in the Nineteenth Century* (Baton Rouge, Louisiana, 1998); R. Graham, 'Causes for the abolition of Negro slavery in Brazil: An interpretive essay', *Hispanic American Historical Review* 46 (1966), pp. 123–37 and 'Brazilian slavery re-examined: A review article', *Journal of Social History* 3 (1970), pp. 431–53.

61. S. Miers, *Slavery in the Twentieth Century: The Evolution of a Global Problem* (Walnut Creek, California, 2003).

62. O. N. Bolland, 'Systems of domination after slavery: The control of land and labor in the British West Indies after 1838', *Comparative Studies in Society and History* 23 (1981), pp. 591–619, esp. 612–17.

63. H. Altink, 'Slavery by another name: Apprenticed women in Jamaican workhouses in the period 1834–8', *Social History* 26 (2001), pp. 40–59, esp. p. 58.

64. W. Kloosterboer, *Involuntary Labour Since the Abolition of Slavery* (Leiden, 1960); D. Eltis (ed.), *Coerced and Free Migration: Global Perspectives* (Stanford, California, 2002).

65. P. Morgan, 'Work and culture: The task system and the world of Lowcountry blacks, 1700 to 1880', *William and Mary Quarterly*, 3rd ser., 39 (1982), pp. 563–99.

66. M. Kale, *Fragments of Empire: Capital, Slavery and Indian Indentured Labor Migration in the British Caribbean* (Philadelphia, Pennsylvania, 1998).

67. J. D. Smith (ed.), *Black Soldiers in Blue: African American Troops in the Civil War Era* (Chapel Hill, North Carolina, 2002); V. DeSantis, 'Rutherford B. Hayes and the removal of the troops and the end of reconstruction', in *Region, Race and Reconstruction: Essays in Honor of C. Vann Woodward* (1982), pp. 417–50; O. Singletary, *Negro Militia and Deconstruction* (Westport, Connecticut, 1984).

68. W. A. Green, 'The planter class and British West Indian sugar production before and after emancipation', *Economic History Review*, 2nd ser., 26 (1973), pp. 448–63, esp. pp. 462–3.

69. P. J. Cain, 'Economics and empire: The metropolitan context', in A. Porter (ed.), *The Oxford History of the British Empire*, III, *The Nineteenth Century* (Oxford, 1999), pp. 34–5.

70. E. Alpers, *Ivory and Slaves in Central Africa* (London, 1975); A. Sheriff, *Slaves, Spices and Ivory in Zanzibar* (London, 1987); T. Ricks, 'Slaves and slave traders in the Persian Gulf, 18th and 19th centuries: An assessment', in W. G. Clarence-Smith (ed.), *The Economics of the Indian Ocean Slave Trade in the Nineteenth Century* (London, 1989), pp. 60–70.

71. R. Coupland, *The Exploitation of East Africa, 1856–90: The Slave Trade and the Scramble* (London, 1939).

72. S. J. Braidwood, *Black Poor and White Philanthropists: London Blacks and the Foundation of the Sierra Leone Settlement, 1786–1791* (Liverpool, 1994).

CHAPTER 5

1. E. Williams, *Capitalism and Slavery* (Chapel Hill, North Carolina, 1944).

2. S. W. Mintz and R. Price, *The Birth of African American Culture: An Anthropological Perspective* (Boston, Massachusetts, 1992).

3. R. Scheck, *Hitler's African Victims. The German Army Massacres of Black French Soldiers in 1940* (Cambridge, 2006), p. 147.

4. F. M. Snowden, *Before Color Prejudice: An Ancient View of Blacks* (Cambridge, Massachusetts, 1983).